52 SABBATHS

UNWRAPPING THE GIFT OF GOD'S REST

A WEEKLY DEVOTIONAL

DAVID HOFFBRAND

Cover design by Ian Barnard

CONTENTS

For all those in need of Sabbath rest

'They must realize that the Sabbath is the Lord's gift to you.' (Exodus 16:29 NLT)

INTRODUCTION

'Then Jesus *said to them, "'The Sabbath was made to meet the needs of people and not people to meet the requirements of the Sabbath.'"*

— MARK 2:27 (NLT)

The Sabbath is one of the most precious, but also most neglected gifts, that God has given to us. We often focus on the second half of what Jesus said - that we shouldn't focus on legalistic observance - and forget that in the first half he was *endorsing,* not dismissing, the Sabbath! And if Jesus tells us something was made to meet our needs, we neglect it at our peril.

The Sabbath is actually one of the greatest keys God has given us for living fruitful lives, and this series of reflections is all about rediscovering its relevance for us today.

Whilst it starts with this idea of a pause or a rest,

when we start to unwrap it we will find that the Sabbath is more like a Swiss army knife, made to meet many of our different needs. So each reflection will look at a different aspect or principle and see how we can apply it in our lives.

The week is often about *speed* of life. The Sabbath is more about *direction*.

IT IS about re-orienting our lives towards the things and relationships that are most *important* (not necessarily most *urgent*). This principle is at the heart of 52 Sabbaths.

Let's start with this - *What actually is the Sabbath?*

God told His people to *'do no ordinary work'* on the seventh day. The Sabbath is like a holiday.

Traditionally Jewish holidays begin at sunset one day and end at sunset on the next, so the Sabbath runs from sunset on Friday to sunset on Saturday.

Jewish people typically prepare everything in the home so they are ready to enter the Sabbath. Just before sunset they light two candles, then once the sun has set they enact a simple ritual taking bread and wine.

The wine represents God's goodness, and the two loaves of bread represent the double portion of manna that God provided for the children of Israel each

Sabbath in the wilderness. They say prayers, acknowledging God's greatness and thanking Him for His provision and for the Sabbath itself.

The aim is to enter the *spirit* of the Sabbath, to recognise that *the next twenty-four hours represent a different way of living and a different mindset.*

That is the heart of it. It is a block of time that is 'set apart', or holy. Yet contained in this simple idea there are principles that can transform our lives, our families and our communities.

Why did God link so many of His blessings to the Jewish people to their continuing practice of the Sabbath? Is He just a stickler for the rules?! No! God told Moses to tell the Israelites, *'They must realize that the Sabbath is the Lord's gift to you.'* (Exodus 16:29 NLT). Too often people have seen it as a ritual to be observed rather than a gift to be unwrapped.

In the same way that the operating system of a computer periodically cleans up the disc space so the machine can run more efficiently, the Sabbath helps us rebalance and reconfigure our lives.

IT TAKES a bit of time but *saves* time in the long run and stops the machine overloading or wearing out, keeping its energies focused on the most important tasks.

When Jesus said *the Sabbath was made for man not man for the Sabbath,* He was not delivering a new truth. He was reminding the people of the principle that God had spoken through Moses - *the Sabbath is a gift from God.* I want to unpack the gift for you!

Each week you will find a new reflection to help you not only discover the meaning and purpose of the Sabbath, but also feed a deeper sense of joy and intimacy in your relationship with God.

I realise that for some people Saturday is a work-day, so the practicalities may look different. If that is the case for you then don't worry - the principles remain the same, but I encourage you to apply them to your individual circumstances in a way that works for you.

The traditional Jewish greeting on the Sabbath is '*Shabbat Shalom*!' - *Shabbat* is the Jewish word for the Sabbath, and *shalom* means peace, wholeness, well-being. I pray these reflections help you enter into a greater sense of God's amazing shalom!

1. GOD

'For in six days the Lord made heaven and earth, but on the seventh day he stopped working and was refreshed.'

— EXODUS 31:17 (NLT)

For in six days the Lord made the heavens, the earth, the sea, and everything in them; but on the seventh day he rested. That is why the Lord blessed the Sabbath day and set it apart as holy.'

— EXODUS 20:11 (NLT)

We must start with this - It is God who gave us the Sabbath *for our benefit*.

God is our example and the first thing He did after creation was take a Sabbath rest. He experienced it Himself, then He gave it to us as a gift. *If He saw value in*

5

it then so must we. However we feel, no matter what has impacted us during the week, and whatever work is left undone, the Sabbath is something that we all need.

The Bible tells us that we are made in God's image. This means that *He has designed us with the Sabbath in mind.*

Regardless of how fruitful our lives, families, or even ministries seem to be, without the Sabbath we are not operating in the fullness of life that God has for us. The Sabbath completes our week.

IF GOD SAID He has set this day apart as holy we know it is precious to Him and He is personally invested in it. He wants to do something *in us* through the Sabbath.

Many of God's commandments call us to change responses that stem from our brokenness, that run counter to His loving nature. But *the Sabbath is a commandment we wrestle with more through neglect.* The challenge is to fully embrace it as God intends us to.

No other society at the time of the Bible had a day off written into their culture. There was a sense that life was a daily struggle, with no time to waste. God specifically told the children of Israel to observe the Sabbath as a declaration that they were now *His* people.

It spoke of a new kingdom that God was establishing on the earth, a new people. And it still does today.

It is countercultural, stepping outside of the race to achieve and dominate for a time every week. It is a practical expression of stepping into the life God has provided for us.

IT IS a revolutionary way of thinking if we embrace it as God intends. And we can choose to enter fully into it every week!

The amazing thing is that the benefits and blessings are not simply for the Sabbath itself, but flow into every part of our lives and the rest of our week.

Think of it like this - when you buy something it often comes with operating instructions. And depending on what personality you are, you might only give these a quick read. But when you get something really expensive you are probably a lot more careful to follow the instructions!

Our lives are more valuable than anything the world has to offer, anything we could ever own. And *the Sabbath is a key part of the operating instructions!* Without it we break, and often end up back with the manufacturer for repair! How much more sensible to follow the instructions in the first place? How much more blessed and fruitful we will be if we accept this offer of weekly maintenance for our lives?

———

When Jesus said, 'The Sabbath was made for man,' He was talking about everyone – that includes you and me, however busy we are.

———

THE SABBATH WAS MADE *for all of us.* If you struggle to really stop on the Sabbath, this is for you. Let's take some time to appreciate and reflect on this gift from God and ask ourselves why He sees it as so vital for our lives.

Through the course of the series we will address different aspects of how we enter into the Sabbath, but this initial reflection is about developing our heart attitude so we begin to place the same value on it that God does.

A good starting place for us is this thought – the Sabbath is a gift to us from a loving Father who wants the best for us and contends to bring us into fruitfulness.

SHABBAT SHALOM

———

REFLECTION:

How do you feel about the Sabbath?

Does it fill you with joy or anxiety about taking 'time out'?

Do you feel guilty or grateful?

Release your feelings to God and ask Him to reveal His heart in the Sabbath.

2. TRUST

'*The Lord is my shepherd I lack nothing, He makes me lie down in green pastures, He leads me beside quiet waters*'

— PSALM 23:1,2 (NLT)

We don't stop on the Sabbath because we have finished. We stop because we acknowledge that whatever work we are doing, whatever responsibilities we have during the week, we are primarily not leading but being led.

We are not carrying but being carried. The Sabbath is a practical step we can take to develop our trust in God.

Maybe you are someone who finds stopping hard. I think many of us can be like this. That's why God gives us a *decision in advance*, a rhythm to stick to. We place our lives back in His hands. Our work will continue later but now we commit everything into His hands and enter into *His* finished work.

We stop what we have been doing to remind our restless souls that we can trust Him, and to develop this trust.

PSALM 23 HAS a particular importance for Jewish people on Shabbat. It is specifically recited during the final meal of the Sabbath (as well as sometimes at the other meals), as though a reminder to our souls before we exit the Sabbath - *this is the One in whom I should place my trust as I step into this week.*

Paul said this: *'And I am certain that God, who began the good work within you, will continue his work until it is finally finished on the day when Christ Jesus returns'* (Philippians 1:6 NLT)

Through the Sabbath we put our trust back in the work God is doing in us.

If we don't, we tend to lose the balance and feel that everything revolves around our own efforts. This is a recipe for stress. Trust is the antidote, and the Sabbath is one of the best means to develop this.

The psalmist reminded the Jewish people *'We are his people, the sheep of His pasture'* (Psalm 100:3 NLT), an image repeated many times throughout the Bible. When Jesus said *'I am the good shepherd'* he was using this image they were familiar with, and specifically making reference to something the prophet Ezekiel talked about (see Ezekiel 34).

The Good Shepherd will not lead us astray, He will protect his sheep, He will take us into good things He has promised. But we must choose to trust Him and allow ourselves to be led.

IT IS no coincidence that so many of the leaders God used were previously shepherds - Moses, David, Jacob's sons, who became the founders of the twelve tribes of Israel.

Our idea of a modern day shepherd is simply someone who looks after a flock of animals. But shepherds in the Bible had to find food, water, and shelter for their flocks in the midst of challenging terrain and fierce climates, to protect them against dangerous wild animals and people who might try to steal them. They needed to be bold, resourceful, and courageous!

This is the kind of shepherd God uses and the kind He is to us. He is a shepherd through all conditions and every trial we may face.

Psalm 23 says *'The Lord is my shepherd; I shall not want. He makes me lie down in green pastures; He leads me beside the still waters'* (Psalm 23:1,2 NKJV).

I think if I am honest, I sometimes allow Him to lead me to those green pastures, and a lot of the time I feel like I am trying to plough my own way through life's weed-filled, rocky terrain, in the hope that something will one day grow there.

When I hit challenges, I try to overcome them in my own strength first rather than trusting in God's leading. The Sabbath reminds me to put my trust in God again in the midst of every struggle or challenge.

When we place our trust in someone it makes us vulnerable to them – they can let us down, fail to do what they say, or misuse that trust.

When we choose to celebrate the Sabbath we are training ourselves to place our trust in the only absolute surefire place we can - God will not let us down, even when things don't seem to be happening the way we would like.

AND IF THINGS are not going according to plan what is our response – continue our efforts to turn things around, try harder to make it better? This Sabbath, let's instead step into this place of rest and say – '*I'm going to trust you Lord! I give it all to you!*'

SHABBAT Shalom

REFLECTION:

HOW DOES it make you feel when you think of placing your life and work back in God's hands? How much do you trust Him?

DOES the level of intimacy you experience with God help you to trust Him or do you need to go deeper this week?

WHAT CAN HELP you to do that?

3. PERSPECTIVE

'But those who trust in the Lord will find new strength.
They will soar high on wings like eagles.'

— ISAIAH 40:31 (NLT)

*One of the great things about the Sabbath is that it helps us
gain and regain God's perspective on our lives.*

In the story of the children of Israel we see that
twelve spies were sent into the promised land and all
saw the same things. Yet two read the situation
differently to the other ten. Why? *Perspective!* Ten saw
the people, giants, and lush crops through the eyes of
fear and thought *The land is great but the people are too
strong for us!* Two saw the same people and crops
through the eyes of faith and thought *The land is great
and the people are our bread! God is giving it to us!*

Which ones were right? All of them were – the ones
who thought they couldn't, couldn't, and the ones who

thought they could, could! This is so true in our lives too.

It was not what they saw that really mattered, it was what they *measured it against*!

Ten measured against their own fears and insecurities, against the lies and oppression they had lived with so long in Egypt, against the chains of the past. The Bible says this caused them to see themselves as grasshoppers. Joshua and Caleb measured instead against the truth of who God was to them and who *He* said they were! Because of this they came up with a different plan.

Your perspective determines your outcome more than your circumstances.

THE INSTRUMENTS we use to measure our lives and the lives of others are not perfect. They have been shaped by our past, and they are affected by our day to day experiences and our culture too. The lens becomes blurred, the surface becomes warped, particles of dirt and dust get trapped in the mechanism. The filter we look through becomes distorted, even very dark sometimes.

Because of this we can lose accuracy in how we measure. This impacts the way we see ourselves and others, and the decisions we make.

If we do not reset and get God's perspective again then these instruments will eventually take us off the course of God's intended destination for our lives.

A couple of degrees can take us a very long way wide of the target if we continue on the same trajectory for too long. We start to compare ourselves to others instead of listening to God's voice. We measure our success by goals God has never set us.

For instance, if we measure our lives against the unreal perfection of someone else's social media feed, then we will always be looking at ourselves with a warped perspective. And we will never be happy. In today's world where we can see into other people's lives in ways never even dreamt of previously, the temptation to do this is greater than ever. Instead,

---

We need the only perspective that really matters on our lives - God's. The Sabbath is our weekly course correction.

THE WAY TO experience this is to wait on Him and rise up as an eagle. Eagles have amazing vision, but they can only use this fully when they are soaring. When we are on the ground surrounded by our challenges and problems we can be overwhelmed and barely see a way forward. Yet as we allow God to take us soaring we can see with His perspective. This, and only this, is the true way to measure our lives.

The Sabbath gives us a space to do this. It is a great time to unplug ourselves from some of the sources of these wrong perspectives that take us off track.

So this Sabbath let's take some time to look up, as we wait on God and let Him lift us to see with His perspective.

SHABBAT SHALOM

REFLECTION:

TAKE time this Sabbath to ask God to give you His perspective on everything, to see it through His eyes, including your self-image and especially any challenges you are facing.

PRACTICAL:

THE SABBATH IS a great opportunity to switch off each week from sources that feed our insecurities and distort our sense of self. What do you need to switch off from this week?

4. LOVE

'Since it was the Sabbath, Jesus' enemies watched him closely. If he healed the man's hand, they planned to accuse him of working on the Sabbath. Jesus said to the man with the deformed hand, "Come and stand in front of everyone." Then he turned to his critics and asked, "Does the law permit good deeds on the Sabbath, or is it a day for doing evil? Is this a day to save life or to destroy it?" But they wouldn't answer him. He looked around at them angrily and was deeply saddened by their hard hearts. Then he said to the man, "Hold out your hand." So the man held out his hand, and it was restored! At once the Pharisees went away and met with the supporters of Herod to plot how to kill Jesus.'

— MARK 3:2-5 (NLT)

Jesus showed them that it was right to do good on the Sabbath, but he didn't tell them to ignore or abolish it.

He was angry because they fixated so much on the details of religious observance that they had missed the very *purpose* of the Sabbath, and therefore misrepresented the loving heart of God.

You see, the rabbis understood that there would be times when God's commandments would seemingly contradict each other. This can be an alien thought to our western mindset, where we like to simply know what is right or wrong. But it's vital if we want to understand what God expects of us, and how Jesus and His disciples thought.

In order to determine what we can/should do in a specific scenario, the rabbis understood that we have to weigh up which commands are 'heavier', or more important, than others.

This helped them to *bind* and *loose* – ie to determine what was permitted or forbidden in any given situation. And these judgments helped people apply God's commands to specific situations.

In this case, we are commanded to rest on the Sabbath, yet we are also commanded to love others as ourselves, and to show mercy.

Jesus reminded the Pharisees that the 'heaviest' or most important commandment is the call to love. This is the lens through which we need to see all our obedience.

IN FACT, in Judaism there is a principle called *pikuach nefesh*, or '*to save a life*'. The idea is that the preservation of life and health overrides any form of religious observance. My father, for example, is a haematologist, and was dealing with life and death situations throughout his working life. He had to go to the hospital most Saturday mornings as part of this responsibility.

So Jesus wasn't telling the religious leaders they were wrong to consider the Sabbath important - he was telling them they were wrong to see it through the lens of legalism rather than love. From this perspective healing fits perfectly on the Sabbath.

Psalm 23:6 (NLT) says, '*Surely your goodness and unfailing love will pursue me all the days of my life*'.

Whatever the other days of our lives have been like, and however busy, on the Sabbath we can allow ourselves to be caught by God's healing love.

JESUS SAID to his disciples '*Freely you have received, freely give*'. So the more we experience of God's love - healing, restoring, and transforming us - the more we can share it with others. And the great thing is - no one else can limit how much of God's love we receive, because *we* determine how open our hearts will be.

The Pharisees got it so wrong they wanted to kill

Jesus! That's extreme! But the truth is that legalism - religion without relationship and rules without reason - always leads to death of some sort rather than life, on the inside and the outside.

As we go on our Sabbath journey it is good to have this foundation, so we don't make the same mistake as the Pharisees. As Jesus reminded them -

---

The ultimate purpose of the Sabbath is not inactivity but love!

THE DISCIPLES of Jesus carried this teaching on. Paul said to Timothy *'The purpose of my instruction is that all believers would be filled with love that comes from a pure heart, a clear conscience, and genuine faith.'* (I Timothy I:5 NLT).

So as we enter this week's Sabbath let's remind ourselves that the ultimate goal of the Sabbath is to help us to love and be loved. The rest is detail.

SHABBAT SHALOM

REFLECTION:

IN WHAT WAYS do you find yourself applying the Bible out of fear rather than love?

IN WHAT AREAS do you need to open yourself to God's love more fully?

HOW CAN you yourself experience God's love more so you can give it out more?

5. REST

'Then Jesus said, "Come to Me, all of you who are weary and carry heavy burdens, and I will give you rest."'

— MATTHEW 11:28 (NLT)

We read in Hebrews 4:9 that there is a special or literally a '*Sabbath rest*' that God has prepared for His people, which we can enter through the finished work of Jesus on the cross.

It is from this place of rest that we are called to live our lives. '*For he who has entered His rest has himself ceased from his works as God did from His*'.

Some people have understood this to mean that because Jesus is our Sabbath rest in this overarching sense, we no longer need an *actual* Sabbath. Yet the Sabbath was kept by Jesus' disciples after he had left, and it is still referred to in prophecies relating to the future.

If we set it aside we miss the point. Do our bodies no longer need rest because we have entered the finished work of Jesus on the cross? Does God really want us to ignore the many benefits that his gift can give us as we find his rhythms for lives, for our families and communities?

'*Remember the Sabbath day, to keep it holy*' is the fourth of the Ten Commandments. It takes up a quarter of the sixteen verses they occupy. It is central to God's vision of the way we are to live! We no longer need live in fear of getting it wrong, but let's not throw out the baby with the bathwater. Because we still need the baby!

The command to rest is good for our bodies, our souls, our spirits, and our families. The rhythm of rest is a blessing for our communities.

THE SERMON on the Mount is all about going beyond the minimum. No one thinks because of the cross that we can murder and commit adultery! Jesus' whole message is that the outward must be a reflection of a deep inner transformation, a wholeheartedness that he is making possible for us.

For instance, Jesus tells us that getting hung up on exact amounts to give is missing the point of wholehearted giving to God. But in doing that He isn't telling us we don't need to give! The opposite.

So, with the Sabbath, I don't think Jesus, or the author of Hebrews, means that we should dismiss the Sabbath. It is more about the profound nature of how we can enter into the rest God has for us.

How do we rest well? What do we rest from? From reliance on our own works. From our need to win acclaim or favour from others, to construct abstract meaning or self-worth for ourselves.

THE REST we have on the Sabbath goes beyond the absence of work. God wants to use it to teach us more about this profound sense of rest, and how we can carry it into our daily living.

The Father said of Jesus, *'This is my beloved son, in whom I am well pleased, hear Him'*. This represents acceptance, approval and affirmation. We too can receive all three in Him and so live from that place of rest for our souls. We don't have to strive to find or create them somewhere else. *That is true rest.*

Our bodies still benefit from rest! And our souls still benefit from a time of reflection and pulling back from striving. Let's use the gift as God intended it!

. . .

Sʜᴀʙʙᴀᴛ ꜱʜᴀʟᴏᴍ

Rᴇꜰʟᴇᴄᴛɪᴏɴ:

Wʜᴇʀᴇ ᴅᴏ you find yourself striving?

Wʜᴀᴛ ʙᴜʀᴅᴇɴꜱ ᴀʀᴇ ᴡᴇɪɢʜɪɴɢ you down?

Wʜᴇʀᴇ ᴅᴏ you find yourself driven by your needs rather than resting in his love?

Tʜɪꜱ Sᴀʙʙᴀᴛʜ ʟᴇᴛ your soul find its rest in him.

6. FAMILY (1)

'...but the seventh day is a Sabbath day of rest dedicated to the Lord your God. On that day no one in your household may do any work'

— EXODUS 20:10 (NLT)

'On the Sabbath day you must each stay in your place'

— EXODUS 16:29 (NLT)

Having grown up in a Jewish family I can say that the Jewish festivals are firstly and most strongly associated with the home and family. The Passover is eaten at home, as the story of the Exodus is told around the dinner table. At Succot Jewish families build a temporary shelter outside their house, which they will spend time in together (and even sleep in if the weather permits). What happens in the synagogue feels like an extension of what happens at home, not the other way around. Sometimes I think as followers of a Jewish Saviour we need to remind ourselves of that principle.

The Sabbath is primarily a time for each household.

ABRAHAM HESCHEL WAS an amazing Jewish scholar and theologian, and his short book, *The Sabbath*, is a poetic and theological masterpiece which I can highly recommend. I will refer to it sometimes in the reflections. Heschel describes how on the Sabbath God wants us to experience *shalom bayit*, or harmony in the home.

The father is supposed to affirm and bless his children, to express appreciation of his wife. The woman of the house invites the presence and light of God to come as she lights the candles. We remind ourselves that *we are in covenant relationships together*. We take time to appreciate each other.

You may be thinking that doesn't sound like *my* family! Or any family (except maybe a fictional Hollywood one). And it will never be perfect. But God is calling us to be *intentional* about developing this. *It is more than just an absence of conflict.*

I have found the more intentional we are, the more this sense of harmony and family celebration grows. Practice helps!

IT'S one of the reasons God gave His people the *weekly* Sabbath. Life gets busy and this kind of time can be scarce. When the whole family knows they have this Sabbath to look forward to it creates a sense of appreciation and anticipation that is life affirming. The Sabbath is a weekly *practice!*

When we stop finding this love, appreciation and warmth in the families we have (whatever they may look like), we can start to look for it elsewhere. If there are underlying issues the Sabbath can act like a simple form of family therapy, helping to restore an appreciation of one another. Ideally, the Sabbath acts as an ongoing catalyst for healthy family dynamics.

In rabbinic thinking the idea developed that to avoid breaking God's prohibition against working on the Sabbath, the people should go no further than '*a Sabbath day's walk*' from their house (2,000 cubits or about 3/4 of a mile). This is referenced in Acts 1:12 as the distance Jesus and his disciples traveled from the Mount of Olives, for instance.

However, the command in Exodus 16:29 was simply

to '*stay in your place*'. To me the core of this is to remain where we are with those closest to us.

The community of God is built from the centre outwards. The revolution of God's kingdom coming to earth does not begin on a battleground but in our individual lives and then our families.

GOD BEGAN the realignment and redemption of His creation with a family – Abram's family. He changed their direction and their purpose. The Sabbath forces us to address the harmony of the family or lack of it. Things we can avoid during the busyness of the week become apparent in the tranquillity of the Sabbath. There are fewer distractions.

Sometimes it is easier to give contributions to humanitarian work happening in other countries, or even to sow our time into different ministries within a church. These are both wonderful things, but *our first call and ministry is to the members of our family*.

God gives us this gift of time as a window to help us create and maintain flourishing families that will withstand the tests of life. When we use the gift right, however we can, it can help us to do exactly that!

So this Sabbath let's be intentional about taking time with our family, whatever that looks like.

Sometimes that simple decision to spend time together each week can have a profound impact on the relationships we are developing and the culture of our families.

SHABBAT SHALOM

REFLECTION:

WHAT CAN you do and what adjustments do you need to make to develop this sense of family celebration on the Sabbath?

7. MEAL

'And people should eat and drink and enjoy the fruits of their labour, for these are gifts from God'

— ECCLESIASTES 3:13 (NLT)

After prayers over the wine and bread, we have the Shabbat meal. According to Jewish tradition there are actually supposed to be a minimum of three meals on the Sabbath (Feel free to have more!).

In the busyness of the week meals can end up being quite functional. It is a precious thing that everyone comes together for the Sabbath meals, especially the one on Friday night.

The Sabbath is not a pitstop to replenish and then race off -

it is a holiday and a celebration, so the Friday Shabbat meal is a feast.

IN JEWISH THINKING there is not a simple dualistic separation between 'spiritual' and 'natural' things. It is not an ascetic religion that sees worldly things as inherently bad or contaminating and supposedly spiritual things as transcendent. God is seen in all aspects of life and all blessings flow from Him. Our humanity is celebrated.

David says in Psalm 27:13 (NKJV) *'I would have lost heart, unless I had believed I would see the goodness of the Lord in the land of the living'*. We can experience God's goodness here and now. It is not just for 'one day', and not all of it is just seen in obviously spiritual things.

The biblical Jewish festivals involve all the senses, and the Sabbath is no exception. Our most profound memories and associations are created when all of our being is involved. God did not create us the way he did by accident.

In Judaism it is actually forbidden to fast on Shabbat. There are some twenty-eight optional fast days but only one is obligatory – the Day of Atonement (Yom Kippur). If any other fast day falls on the Sabbath it is postponed until the next day.

It runs counter to our normal religious thinking to think that fasting on the Sabbath is generally considered wrong, whereas to feast is considered biblical and righteous, based on such verses as Isaiah's injunction to '*call the Sabbath a delight*'.

A meal speaks of celebration, of relationship and love, and especially so in biblical times. Hospitality is a core part of Middle Eastern culture. To share a meal is to share life.

JESUS HIMSELF EVEN SAID, '*Look! I stand at the door and knock. If you hear my voice and open the door, I will come in, and we will share a meal together as friends.*' (Revelation 3:20 NLT). He isn't talking about just grabbing a sandwich during a lunchbreak. He is talking about a covenant relationship and sharing of life.

Typically a Sabbath meal is not a time to rush, it is a time to relax, to communicate, to share, perhaps process the victories and the challenges of the week. Even let go of disappointments and failures.

It is said that it is a sin to be sad on the Sabbath. Sometimes we cannot help it, but it is a good, life enhancing principle. Meals help!

Indeed, the rabbis consider the Sabbath to be a taste of eternity. And eternity starts with a feast and celebration, described in the Bible in terms of a wedding supper. Jesus likened the Gospel to an invitation to a banquet.

The bedrock of who we are is expressed in this Sabbath meal, the central covenant relationships of our life – God, close family, and friends. We share a meal. We share our lives.

FOR US AS a family with very young children it is not always easy to all eat together. Sometimes we do, but often children are eating earlier and we are busy sorting things out still. Sometimes the meal together becomes a Saturday brunch!

Yet we try to build this sense of coming back together on Friday night, of gathering around food, the bread and wine, acknowledging this as family time. And the older they get the more we will build this sense of a family celebration and a meal together.

So consider this week what that time looks like for you. Be intentional.

SHABBAT Shalom

PRACTICAL:

WHAT DOES your Friday night look like?

IS it the same as every night?

HOW CAN you make this meal special, more like a feast, to create a sense of celebration and anticipation for all the family?

8. COMMUNITY

'Behold how good and pleasant it is for brethren to dwell together in unity'

— PSALM 133:1 (NKJV)

The Sabbath is not an individual occupation. The commandment explicitly lists all those who are to celebrate it -

'but the seventh day is a Sabbath day of rest dedicated to the Lord your God. On that day no one in your household may do any work. This includes you, your sons and daughters, your male and female servants, your livestock, and any foreigners living among you.'

— EXODUS 20:9,10 (NLT)

THE SABBATH IS integral to community. It is a shared experience that reminds us we are not just individuals saved by God, but a community being shaped by Him.

God sent one man, Moses, to bring the children of Israel out of Egypt so they could be His *people*, His representatives. The commands He gave them afterwards outlined what this community should look like.

God sent His Son Jesus and called us out of our Egypt to become a people, a community together. The Sabbath is not reserved for certain individuals or sections of society, it is a reminder that we have been brought by Him into a new community that is likened to a body, a family (composed of Jewish and Gentile followers of Jesus together).

There are different elements to the Sabbath. There is that sense of personal rest and reflection, as well as reconnecting with God. But -

---

The Sabbath is a time for building relationships with others in the community, outside of the pressures of everyday work.

ROUTINE CAN SWALLOW up our appreciation for others, and even our recognition of our *need* for others. The Sabbath reminds us and gives us a space for this.

On other days we may be too tired from work. We may be too preoccupied or busy. But God clears our diaries once a week like the ultimate concerned personal assistant and says – in this space just consider Me, yourself, and your relationships with others.

On working days we are brought into contact with others by what we are doing. On the Sabbath we are choosing to connect with others and build relationships that will enhance our lives and theirs.

If you go to Israel you will find a question repeatedly asked of you by both religious and non-religious Jews – *'Where are you going for Shabbat?'* There is a deep, shared understanding that the Sabbath is not the time for people to be alone. It is implicitly understood that the Sabbath is a feast is to be celebrated with others, family first but extending outwards also.

It is not good for the man to be alone (Gen. 2:18 NLT) – was God's thought before He created Eve in Genesis. *God sets the solitary in families (Psalms 68:6 NKJV),* according to the Psalmist. Paul describes how the whole body of believers is being *'joined and knit together',* in love (Eph. 4:16 NKJV).

God takes great care to ensure that we are becoming not just individually fulfilled, but part of a growing and healthy community.

We live in a society that prizes the rights and needs of the individual more than any before. We can so often read the Bible through this lens – as though it were written for us as individuals alone, like a self-help book. In reality the Bible is written to you plural or '*us*', not to you singular or '*me*'.

This is especially true of the New Testament. As English readers we must remember that most of the 'you's in the New Testament are plural. Paul wrote his letters to whole communities of believers identified by their location. The letters would have been read aloud to them all together.

On the Sabbath we appreciate the fellowship of God, but also celebrate the fellowship of those who do life alongside us. We are reminded that we are not alone, however it may seem.

Loneliness is one of the most insidious and debilitating diseases of modern societies. It is a poison and the Sabbath is supposed to be part of the antidote, as relevant today as it ever was.

I think if we are part of a fellowship or church of some kind, we can almost assume this means we are actively involved in community, even if all we are doing is attending meetings. Although this is great, the

Sabbath is a space for developing the kinds of friendships that put real meat on the bones of what community actually means. Community is built one relationship at a time.

So this Sabbath let's build relationships and develop community. It is good for our souls.

SHABBAT SHALOM

PRACTICAL:

WHO ARE you with on the Sabbath? Who are you actively building relationship with? Who is your community?

9. WORK (1)

'The Lord God placed the man in the Garden of Eden to tend and watch over it.'

— GENESIS 2:15 (NLT)

Work was not a curse! Nor is it incidental. The Jewish theologian Abraham Heschel said in his book, The Sabbath, 'Labour is not only the destiny of man; it is endowed with divine dignity'. This means that -

The curse was not work, it was in our relationship to our work. We don't need to be set free from work, but from the curse.

Adam was called to work in partnership with God, who walked and talked with him. He was to work in rhythm with God, in pace, in time, in heart, in step. Not hounded or oppressed by work. The curse is described in Genesis 3:17 (NKJV) - 'in toil shall you eat... all the days *of your life'* – so as Heschel points out, *toil* is the curse, not work.

The word translated *toil* is the Hebrew word *issabon*, which means pain, hardship, distress, sorrow, or toil. The word for Adam's original tending of the garden is *abad*, meaning to serve, worship, minister –

God calls us to labour and minister with Him. Work is not inherently sorrowful or hardship. Our work can be an act of worship.

THE INTIMACY and joy of Adam's initial call contrasts with the work the children of Israel ended up doing in Egypt as Pharaoh's slaves. This work *does* represent the curse. It is a vivid example of work not as a blessing and a joy, but as a source of misery and oppression. It had no end, no rest to look forward to or celebrate.

When God brought the children of Israel out of Egypt, he reminded them of the Sabbath, and told them it would be a key marker to differentiate them from all other peoples.

The Sabbath was a reminder that they were now God's free people, not working as slaves but working in covenant partnership with Him.

We don't live or work without goals or a destination.

The Sabbath is firstly a weekly reminder that God himself is, just as he told Abraham, our ultimate reward. The Sabbath doesn't prepare us to work, so much as our work prepares and leads us to the Sabbath. This is just as it was with God at creation. The rabbis liken the Sabbath to a taste of our ultimate union with God.

We are heading for peace. For joy. For love. We don't fight helplessly, as Paul said, *'as ones who beat the air'*. We are never without purpose or direction. All our work is preparing us for this union with our God. To enter that rest he has for us and is for us. We are led not driven.

Secondly, the Sabbath helps us separate *toil* from the work God intends for us. Paul said *'do all things as unto the Lord'*.

Work is not a nuisance from which we need to be liberated. It is a partnership with God that we can embrace, so long as we know the one with whom and for whom we are working.

TO DIVIDE up our lives into secular (our weekdays) and spiritual (our Sundays) is to miss the sense that God himself has given us a rhythm, a pattern. *Our work is spiritual too.*

The Sabbath ensures, however, that our work does

not become our sorrow or our idol. We remember that we serve the creator not the creation. We are the clay not the potter.

The Sabbath redeems our work by keeping it in its rightful place.

Only when we re-evaluate our work in this manner are we truly liberated from the curse of sorrow and toil and instead relate to our work as God intended. Whatever work we are doing we can do in partnership with the Creator Himself.

Work is not a distraction from our calling. It is a fundamental part of it! Viewed in this light our work helps us to become who we are called to be. So this Sabbath let's take some time to re-evaluate our concept of work, and our relationship to it.

SHABBAT SHALOM

REFLECTION:

WHAT IS your relationship to your work - are you free to serve in it, or does it seem to control and burden you?

IS WORK a joy or a sorrow to you?

. . .

Do you feel like you need to be liberated from it, or do you work in partnership with God as you serve Him in your world?

10. WORK (2)

'Six days you shall labor and do all your work, but the seventh day is the Sabbath of the Lord your God.'

— DEUTERONOMY 5:13 (NKJV)

'It is good for people to eat, drink, and enjoy their work under the sun during the short life God has given them..'

— ECCLESIASTES 5:18 (NLT)

It is true that when we step back and rest each week we can accomplish our work more effectively than if we just worked every single day. But this is not the main aim of the Sabbath.

Abraham Heschel says – *'Man is not a beast of burden,*

and the Sabbath is not for the purpose of enhancing the efficiency of his work.' He continues, 'The Sabbath is not for the sake of the weekdays; the weekdays are for the sake of the Sabbath. It is not an interlude but the climax of living' (Heschel, The Sabbath, p14). The idea of 'living for the weekend' is older than we think!

The Sabbath is not defined by a passive inactivity, but by a different kind of activity.

WE MAY NOT DO our *'ordinary work'* – the work of dominating and making our way in the world. But this absence is to make room for something else – the nurturing of our soul and relationships.

We do not even need to think about our normal work. Rather we feed different aspects of our lives. We experience a glimpse of the true life we are ultimately called to live.

The Sabbath has always been this taste of what it means to be redeemed from the curse. The Sabbath pre-dated the Torah commandments given to the people of Israel. It pre-dated all things except the creation itself.

In Jesus we are not only liberated from the *'curse of the Law'* (ie the guilt that lies on us for our inability to truly keep God's commandments), but from the original curse laid on Adam and Eve. We are restored to a position of intimacy with God.

This means we work from a different mindset -

We don't work for acceptance by others, nor for the world's acclaim. Instead we are called to work from our position as sons and daughters of God. We are not working to prove our worth but to represent God.

We are not working to become something or someone valuable. We are working from a place of security that in God we are *'a royal priesthood...His own special people'* (2 Peter 2:9 NKJV) , and that *'the father Himself loves you'* (John 16:27 NKJV).

On the Sabbath we can let go of our attempts to find security or identity through our work and remind ourselves of these truths. And so we become freer to define and manage our relationship to our work.

PERHAPS WE NEED to take bolder decisions? Perhaps we need to simply bring more life to what we do? The more we step away and reconnect with what is most important to our soul, to the position we already occupy in God's heart, the more light we can carry when we come back.

The Bible affirms the validity and importance of

hard work, of real engagement. It also shows us that like all other things it must be in its proper place. It cannot control us any more than money can. We are led not driven.

The Sabbath helps us place work in its proper context in our lives. We remember to engage as the head and not the tail. Situations that have overwhelmed us in the workplace loosen their hold on our identity as we engage fully with that Sabbath rest.

Paul said *'Not I but the grace of God that labored through me'* – by the grace of God I worked harder... *However hard we work we must remind ourselves that our work is an expression of God's grace working through us, not a way of measuring our value.*

So this Sabbath we let's ask ourselves some honest questions about our work and make sure we are working from the place of acceptance and approval in God.

SHABBAT SHALOM

REFLECTION:

WHAT AM I seeking through my work that I should be looking for in God? Identity? Acclaim?

. . .

WORK (2)

IN WHAT WAYS do I need to redefine my relationship to my work?

11. RIGHTEOUSNESS

Then Jesus said to his critics, "I have a question for you. Does the law permit good deeds on the Sabbath, or is it a day for doing evil? Is this a day to save life or to destroy it?"

— LUKE 6:9 (NLT)

Our idea of righteousness is focused primarily on a spiritual position before God. The Hebrew concept of righteousness is much more closely entwined, however, with *a way of life*.

The Hebrew word translated as righteousness is *Tzedekah*. It refers less to a passive state we exist in than to an actual obligation to act with justice.

A *tzadik*, or righteous person, describes someone who gives to the poor and generally looks out for others who may be in need, especially those in positions of less power and privilege than themselves. It is not passive.

Righteousness in Jewish thought is not exclusively an abstract or legal judgement by God, but also about someone committing to a path of justice and benevolence.

We know that the good deeds we do cannot lead us to justification before God. We are declared righteous through our faith in what Jesus has done for us.

However, the idea of justification by faith does not mean that righteousness amounts *only* to a set of beliefs or an abstract position that God places us in.

Although our righteous deeds cannot lead us to redemption, our redemption can and should lead us to a life that becomes more righteous in its expression.

IN OUR WAY of thinking we may associate *'works'* with the Old Testament, and *'faith'* (as separate from actions) with the New Testament. But consider this –

'The just shall live by their faith' was written to Israelites under the Old Covenant.

The Sermon on the Mount is Jesus' teaching on how to live out the commands of God. John, the apostle of love, later said that to love God is to obey His commands.

James (really a Jewish man called Jacob) said *'What good is it, dear brothers and sisters, if you say you have faith but don't show it by your actions? Can that kind of faith save anyone? ...So you see, faith by itself isn't enough. Unless it produces good deeds, it is dead and useless..'''*

He concludes, 'So you see, we are shown to be right with God by what we do, not by faith alone.' (James 2:24 NLT)

During the week we are often so busy with our 'ordinary work' and family, but the Sabbath gives us a space to consider the good we can do for others.

It is a time when we can consider how to put our faith to work and express righteousness through our actions towards those around us, unhurried by the busyness of life.

It is interesting that more of Jesus' healing miracles took place on the Sabbath than any other day. We too should put our faith to work for the benefit of others as he did, bringing healing where we can.

The Sabbath holds in tension this idea of a position before God – as we enter an unearned rest, a day he has blessed and set apart for us – and the actions we take towards others – as we all rest and develop a heart of compassion.

The Sabbath commandment actually sits at the start

of the last six of the ten commandments, the ones that help us to love others.

So this Sabbath lets develop the active sense of what it means to act in a righteous manner. This might mean inviting a family or someone who is otherwise isolated to your table, or looking to do good to a neighbour.

Whatever it looks like, as Jesus said – the Sabbath is a time for doing good!

SHABBAT SHALOM

REFLECTION:

WHAT IS your idea of righteousness?

WHAT GOOD CAN you do this Sabbath?

12. COMPASSION

'You must not mistreat or oppress foreigners in any way. Remember, you yourselves were once foreigners in the land of Egypt. You must not exploit a widow or an orphan.'

— EXODUS 22:21-24 (NLT)

'Also you shall not oppress a stranger, for you know the heart of a stranger, because you were strangers in the land of Egypt.'

— EXODUS 23:9 (NKJV)

The Sabbath is linked throughout the Bible to a call for justice and compassion. God wants his people to carry his heart, especially for those members of society who are least valued or powerful, and most likely to be oppressed.

The original Sabbath commandment in Exodus 20:10 (NLT) stated that *'no one in your household may do any work. This includes you, your sons and daughters, your male and female servants, your livestock, and any foreigners living among you.'*

In the verses at the top, which follow on from this, God expands on this idea and explains the *why* behind the what -

---

God says you were foreigners in Egypt, so you should understand how to be compassionate as I am - you know the heart of a foreigner.

WHEN YOU LOOK at how the Israelites became slaves in Egypt it is very interesting - they were not captured, but actually became slaves from a place of great blessing and prosperity. It says a new king came to power in Egypt, who knew nothing about Joseph or what he had done.

The more I read the story the more I think that God allowed his people to become slaves precisely *so they would always carry his compassionate heart.*

God requires that we never forget what it is to have

the heart of an alien or stranger - to feel other, excluded, different, less valued, less entitled and provided for.

As Walter Brueggemann puts it in his book, Sabbath as Resistance, neighbourliness is at the heart of God's new community. And neighbours are not only those like us.

This compassion, moreover, cannot be a passive thing. It must result in actions to create more compassionate society.

James (who was actually called Jacob) said '*Pure and genuine religion in the sight of God the Father means caring for orphans and widows in their distress and refusing to let the world corrupt you*' (James 1:27 NLT).

And throughout God's commandments, we are instructed to look out for the interests of those in need or distress, and the strangers amongst us.

This is the new kingdom. It makes friends of the other and extends God's same loving favour to all. The Sabbath is a cornerstone of this.

The Sabbath is a weekly declaration and reminder that God cares for all, and especially looks out for those outcast, broken, and less powerful members of society.

IT FORCES us to consider whether we are the same and carry God's heart and agenda. That refrain should echo within us - *you were once aliens.*

Now you are mine, says God, but I am compassionate. So in remembering *whose* you are you must also become like me. Act with compassion and justice towards those same disenfranchised people in your world that I care for.

This Sabbath let's consider our heart in this area and ask God to help us develop this same sense of compassion.

SHABBAT SHALOM

REFLECTION:

HOW MUCH DO you carry God's heart for the broken and less powerful members of society?

PRAYER:

GOD, help me to remember what it felt like to be a stranger from your kingdom, so that I can carry your heart of compassion towards others.

13. REPAIR

'the Lord has told you what is good, and this is what he requires of you: to do what is right, to love mercy, and to walk humbly with your God.'

— MICAH 6:8 (NLT)

The Gospel is not only focused on our individual salvation but on the coming of the king and his kingdom. Our salvation brings us into freedom but also into partnership with God in building his kingdom, here on the earth.

As Dwight Pryor puts it in his series, Unveiling the Kingdom of Heaven, *'Salvation from a Hebraic point of view is more than the assurance of a place in the world to come; it is a summons in this world to the service of the King'.*

The transformation of society is therefore not the incidental by-product of lots of individually changed lives. It is the central goal of God's vision.

IN RABBINIC JUDAISM there is a concept called Tikkun Olam. It means repairing the world. Keeping the Sabbath is considered one aspect of it.

THIS IDEA RESONATES with God's call to us to build the new kingdom, heaven coming to earth.

Tikkun olam can include prayer, action to repair the environment, acts of kindness, and so on. The heart of it is to accept responsibility for helping to improve the world.

The Bible tells us that we have received the same anointing for the transformation of society that Jesus carried and proclaimed. We are his body, continuing his mission. And he taught us to pray for his kingdom to come on earth.

So even as God works in us, we must let him work through us. We are called to serve the poor. We are to become a voice for the oppressed as he is. In short, we are to work to birth and build this new kingdom community where people are looked after, the homeless housed, the naked clothed, and so on.

We cannot be indifferent to the suffering or exclusion of others.

This is not a side issue but central to the Gospel. It is what the early church community in Acts (all Jewish we must remember) began to enact. And God links the

Sabbath and justice and compassion because it is supposed to keep us on this mission! It is a taste of the kingdom coming on earth.

It is radical, yes. But it is not birthed out of the overthrow of governments or authority. It starts with the overthrow of pride and selfishness, and ultimately self-seeking, in each of our hearts. A quiet revolution that radiates out. Put is this way -

---

You cannot have the Gospel without personal transformation. But you cannot have personal transformation without social transformation and justice.

CHANGE on the inside without change on the outside is not change. Ask my wife! If I say I am changed but don't love more and behave differently then I am not really changed.

Tikkun olam includes acts of worship and prayer that bring a greater awareness of the presence of God into the world. This is part of the repairing. But it also includes any action or activity that impact the communities around us for good. It is the outworking of neighbourliness.

For Jewish people this means prayer, loving friends and family, and so on. But also doing acts of kindness to others, contributing financially to those in need and offering help where we can. Becoming part of the solution.

This Sabbath let's ask ourselves some hard questions. Are we aligning ourselves with this process of *Tikkun olam*? Are we participating in the work of re-making society and re-building community to see his kingdom established, led by his love? This is as much the Gospel as our own personal road to salvation.

So let's decide to partner with God with every fibre of our being.

SHABBAT SHALOM

REFLECTION:

How BIG IS your picture of the Gospel?

How MUCH DO you feel like you are partnering with God in repairing the world?

WHAT CAN you do to further this?

14. NOISE

'Be still and know that I am God'

— PSALM 46:10 (NLT)

He calmed the storm to a whisper
and stilled the waves.

— PSALM 107:29,30 (NLT)

What a blessing was that stillness as he brought them safely into harbor!

In the week we have noise and busyness. On the Sabbath we are invited to quiet and stillness and space. In the endless clamour of modern living these are not natural components of our lifestyle but things we have to practice and schedule.

You might say we become the guest of the Sabbath each week. It is a banquet of time to which we are invited.

Yet in the quiet there is not really quiet, nor stillness in the stillness. The engine of our souls continues to turn over incessantly, with plans and thoughts and worries and ideas.

The silence of the Sabbath gives us the space to hear the noise within.

It is like the engine of a car. There are some obvious noises you can hear when out driving that tell you something is wrong. Clearly wrong. Especially when you're stuck on the side of the road having had a breakdown!

But sometimes it is only when a car goes into the garage and they listen to the engine and examine it, that it becomes apparent there are some odd noises happening. Even the faintest of sounds that is off becomes more audible and apparent.

So it is with us. There may be obvious issues that we encounter in the week that need fixing. Hopefully we don't breakdown altogether.

The Sabbath is like a garage and God is the ultimate mechanic.

Firstly we must bring the car in. Then we must learn to listen with him for those sounds that sound 'off'. In the silence it's harder to kid yourself. That funny noise can't be the road or the other drivers. It's just you. And me.

So as we stand before him each Sabbath we need to just keep an ear peeled for those odd little noises, the rattles that tell us something is not quite right with our engine. Even at rest.

And then we simply need to let the greatest mechanic of them all work on the engine till it is fixed and raring to go.

The stillness of the Sabbath gives us a space to retune, and to hear and acknowledge the noises in our lives that just aren't right.

IT's OK, he knows. He just wants to fix us. Jesus said it's the sick not the well who need a doctor. He is that doctor for our souls. The Sabbath is often his surgery. Let's enter and be changed.

Stillness and silence are our friends.

So this Sabbath, in the midst of celebration and relaxation, take a moment to notice the sounds of the engine. Or even to acknowledge that sound that it has been making all week as you travelled. And let God be the mechanic.

Let the stillness and the silence enter your soul, and God's Spirit with them.

SHABBAT SHALOM

REFLECTION:

WHAT NOISES RECUR in your life that God needs to retune?

HOW DO you feel embracing a little bit of stillness and silence?

PRACTICAL:

TAKE a few minutes somehow and just breathe, listen, acknowledge the sound of the engine. Share it with God.

15. HATS

And because we are his children, God has sent the Spirit of his Son into our hearts, prompting us to call out, "Abba, Father."

— GALATIANS 4:6 (NLT)

As is traditional for Jewish people the men usually wear small head coverings called *yarmulkes* or *Kippurs*. These are supposed to acknowledge God over us. My oldest son, Isaac, used to call them *'challah hats'*.

For a while, Isaac got in the habit of putting a tiny woollen cap from a Scottish themed teddy on our then eleven-month old, Levi, when we lit the candles and prayed together at the start of the Sabbath. It looked so comical and a bit bizarre! We didn't mind because we want them to associate the Sabbath with joy more than solemnity!

In truth, I think most of us are striving a lot of the time to find a hat that fits in life

We're looking for a role, a personality, a way of being, an identity that will suit us and help us function well in the different settings we find ourselves in each week.

Some of them are more subtle and understated. Some look more glaringly obvious and strange to God, and even to others. If truth be told we can all look a little funny sometimes, especially when we try and wear personalities and roles that are not quite us and make them fit! And we've all done it!

On the Sabbath we have a space and an invitation to take off these hats that can become a trap, an accidental mask of our own making.

WHEN WE ENTER the Sabbath we return to our true identity as sons and daughters of God. This is emphasized repeatedly in the Bible. Through the prophet Ezekiel, for instance, God says the Sabbath days are *'a sign to remind you that I am the Lord your God'* (Ezekiel 20:20 NLT).

It is as though we take off the invisible hat we wear in the week and (symbolically) put on the one that truly defines us as we acknowledge God.

All our other identities will disappear or become obsolete one day. But we will always remain sons and daughters of God. The Sabbath is a time to remember and enjoy this.

USUALLY, as Levi flipped around and wriggled, that funny little Scottish hat came off. With practice we can shake these other hats we wear off just as easily.

And in doing this, we are learning to become more like our true selves. And this can hopefully help us stay true to ourselves for the week itself.

It is vital that whatever role we play in the week, we do not allow that to become our fixed identity. That includes even the ministry and calling God has for us.

The Sabbath shouldn't be a time to try and impress anybody. To *'stay in our own place'* should mean to be somewhere where people know and love us just as we are. Hopefully that means family and friends.

This Sabbath, let's loosen our grip as much as possible on any hats we have to wear, and trust in God's covering over our lives.

SHABBAT SHALOM

REFLECTION:

WHAT HATS DO you need to take off this Sabbath?

WHAT DEFINES YOU TOO MUCH, or holds too much sway over your identity, that you need to let go of?

WHAT DO you need to remember about your true identity as a son or daughter of God?

16. THRIVE

'They are like trees planted along the riverbank, bearing fruit each season. Their leaves never wither, and they prosper in all they do.'

— PSALM 1:3 (NLT)

"I am the vine, you are the branches. He who abides in Me, and I in him, bears much fruit;"

— JOHN 15:5 (NKJV)

Life is a struggle. Every day feels like a battle – for achievement, self-esteem, direction, positive relationships – you name it, and it can feel like a struggle. That even goes for ministry too. But -

God has called us to thrive not strive.

Of course, we want to learn how to do this throughout the week. But the Sabbath is a practical lesson in abiding, so we can learn to bear fruit. If we can't do it in a twenty four hour period of rest, the chances are we will struggle in the rush of weekday living.

This is counter-intuitive – we stop working to become more fruitful. Yet that is exactly what God says. He tells us the more we can learn what this looks like, and learn to do it, the more we can bear fruit.

You don't hear trees straining. They are drawing up water from the roots. They are doing what they are designed to do.

WE ARE DESIGNED to be filled with God's Spirit, and to draw off Him. When we do, people see the fruit that grows in our lives as a result. In his letter to the Galatians Paul listed some of the fruit – love, joy, peace, patience, kindness, goodness, faithfulness, gentleness, and self-control. That sounds like someone who is thriving! And Paul says that is just the *kind* of fruit that grows. There is more.

The main transaction is below the surface. The Sabbath is one of the foundations of a healthy life. No one walks past a house and says 'Oh, nice foundations!'.

But the foundations are what enables you to build a great house.

Abiding and resting are similar. They both sound peaceful, effortless, liberating. This is the Sabbath – an exercise in abiding and resting in the blessings God has given us.

In a world consumed with busyness we need to learn this more than ever. That is why people are more interested in the Sabbath than ever. We are re-thinking where we have thrown out the baby of rest with the bathwater of legalism.

The world has its own version of mindfulness and meditation, but God offers us something better than both in our relationship with him. He offers us his Spirit to lead and guide us, and he gives us the Sabbath as a sanctuary in which to practice.

Jesus criticized the Pharisees because they had turned the Sabbath from thrive to strive. This is what he meant when he said that the Sabbath was made for man, not man for the Sabbath.

So this Sabbath, let's aim for – not strive for – that sense of thriving, of abiding, of drawing peacefully from God.

As it says in Psalm 36:7,8 (NLT) –

How precious is your unfailing love, O God! All humanity finds shelter in the shadow of your wings. You feed them from the abundance of your own house, letting them drink from your river of delights. For you are the fountain of life, the light by which we see.

The river keeps flowing and the fountain keeps pouring. God's water is always available to us. We thrive when we stop and draw it up into our lives.

SHABBAT SHALOM

REFLECTION:

IN WHAT WAYS do you feel like you are thriving or striving?

HOW CAN you use the Sabbath rest to learn more about letting go and abiding in God?

17. LISTEN

Then He said, "Go out, and stand on the mountain before the Lord." And behold, the Lord passed by, and a great and strong wind tore into the mountains and broke the rocks in pieces before the Lord, but the Lord was not in the wind; and after the wind an earthquake, but the Lord was not in the earthquake; and after the earthquake a fire, but the Lord was not in the fire; and after the fire a still small voice. So it was, when Elijah heard it, that he wrapped his face in his mantle and went out and stood in the entrance of the cave. Suddenly a voice came to him, and said, "What are you doing here, Elijah?"

— I KINGS 19:11-13 (NKJV)

The week is full of earthquakes, winds, and fires. Yet God usually speaks to us in a whisper. The Sabbath is a time to hear that whisper.

Earthquakes speak of shaking – so much that I

experience can shake me. Shake my confidence, my sense of identity, my purpose.

The devil questioned Eve, *'Did the Lord really say...?'* – an earthquake of doubt.

The trials we face each week can feel like little earthquakes. Sometimes it seems to take so little to destabilise me – someone says the wrong thing, unintentionally usually. Someone having a bad day in a shop is rude to me and I walk away angry at them.

And how easy is it to think we hear God's voice speaking to us in these earthquakes, without even realising it – circumstances challenge us and we allow them to judge us, to make us feel we have somehow missed God's blessing, or whatever other lie that we have internalised.

Winds blow with messages all around us. Society imposes prevailing messages that speak so loudly, trapping us, driving the ship of our life off course.

FIRES RAGE IN OUR HEARTS. Conflicts, both external and internal, can consume all the oxygen in our lives, so that we struggle to breathe and be free as God intended.

Yet our God, the Bible says, is a consuming fire. He is the one who wants us to burn in our hearts with his love.

The verses each time say, *'the Lord was not in the wind...not in the earthquake...not in the fire...'*

These events and circumstances that can suffocate and buffet us are not the voice or judgement of God on our lives. There is something more –

'...after the fire a still small voice.'

I love this picture. After these circumstances that seemed so momentous and overwhelming – a wind, an earthquake, a fire – something comes that is more powerful than all these – the still, small, voice of God.

When we hear the voice of God everything else seems trivial and unimportant by comparison. God's whisper in your heart is louder than every wind, earthquake, or fire that may be raging in your life.

PSALM 29:4 (NKJV) says *'The voice of the Lord is powerful; the voice of the Lord is full of majesty'*. And yet in my experience it comes as a whisper more often than not.

God spoke the universe into being. So he really doesn't need to shout to accomplish his purposes in our lives. The Bible says that faith comes by hearing and hearing by the word of God. It also says that God's word does not return void but accomplishes what it is sent for. So it is vital that we hear him.

The Sabbath is supposed to be a time where we can more easily hear the whisper of God in our lives.

Notice God didn't try to speak over the wind, or the earthquake, or fire. He is not competing but waiting for that moment when the circumstances have made Elijah ready to hear.

ELIJAH WRAPPED his face in his mantle. He covered his mouth, a time to listen more than to speak.

The word for *still* also means *calm*. God brings calm to Elijah. The seemingly huge events don't carry the truth. God's still small voice does. He is not ruffled by the difficult circumstances of our lives. And when he speaks it is such a simple, personal conversation – '*What are you doing here?*' Followed by three very clear instructions.

This Sabbath we have time to let the winds, earthquakes, and fires that have been affecting us all week lead us to a place of listening. In the place of quiet and rest let's step out of our cave, cover our mouths, and allow God's still small voice to bring calm to our souls and set new direction for our lives.

SHABBAT SHALOM

REFLECTION:

WHAT WINDS HAVE BEEN BLOWING you off course this week?

WHAT EARTHQUAKES HAVE BEEN SHAKING your foundations?

WHAT FIRES HAVE BEEN CONSUMING your heart?

PRACTICAL:

TAKE A MOMENT, even five or ten minutes, to listen for that still small voice of peace in your heart, to discern in the silence what God is saying to you.

18. IDOLS

'For they had rejected my regulations, refused to follow my decrees, and violated my Sabbath days. Their hearts were given to their idols.'

— EZEKIEL 20:16 (NLT)

"Then I warned their children not to follow in their parents' footsteps, defiling themselves with their idols. 'I am the Lord your God,' I told them. 'Follow my decrees, pay attention to my regulations, and keep my Sabbath days holy, for they are a sign to remind you that I am the Lord your God.'

— EZEKIEL 20:18-20 (NLT)

The command to observe the Sabbath is designed to constantly draw our hearts back to God and away from our idols. God says the Sabbaths are *'a sign to remind you that I am the Lord your God'*. He knows we need reminding!

The gods of other nations and religions, the gods of the cultures around them - these were always a snare for the Israelites. Again and again they succumbed to the temptation to go after these idols instead of God himself.

What are the idols that our heart goes after *today*? Perhaps they are not those ancient idols drawn from the natural world and old traditions. But there are different kinds of idols which surround us in our culture.

As the verses imply, each generation faces the same challenge - the old idols do not disappear, and new ones are always emerging.

Fame is an idol that can easily draw our heart. No matter how many celebrities say that they have found it miserable or illusory, we can yearn for this sense of being known. But -

---

On the Sabbath we remember that we are already known, by one who truly loves us and lifts us.

MONEY CAN BE an idol that draws our hearts. We consider that if only we have enough we will be satisfied and at ease.

But on the Sabbath we remember that God is Jehovah Jireh, our provider. He even provided a double portion of mannah in the wilderness, so the children of Israel didn't have to gather on the Sabbath. God is our goal, not money.

Power and success can be idols. We can feel that if only we had that position, title, that sway in society, then we would become satisfied.

But on the Sabbath we remember that any power or success we may have is from God. We remember that we are all weak before God, before we are made strong in him. We depend on him. Our only real or lasting title is child of God.

The folk singer, Woody Guthrie, had '*This machine kills fascists*' written on his guitar. His songs were designed to promote and celebrate justice, to call out injustices he saw.

The Sabbath would have '*This machine kills idols*' written on it if it were a guitar! God gave it to us for this purpose. But it only works when we actually use it. And we have to learn, just like Woody Guthrie had to learn to play his guitar.

If each week we come back to dependence on God, and to the

***revelation of his truth, then our idols will increasingly
wither and die. They will lose their grip.***

I don't know what idols exist in your life. I have found
that some in my life are obvious, and some less so. My
heart has gone after so many, and the temptations
remain, fuelled in areas of my own brokenness.

The messages of the culture around me speak loudly
and constantly too, feeding those temptations and
insecurities. We can be easily drawn into seeking
fulfilment and healing in places we cannot truly find
them.

But the Sabbath is a space and a tool to help us let go
of our idols so we can embrace fully who we are in in
him.

God doesn't condemn us. He wants to give us rest.
The Bible says the Holy Spirit brings conviction that
leads to repentance, a change of direction. That is what
we need when it comes to our idols, each week, to keep
us on track and growing strong.

So this Sabbath let's examine our hearts and let go of
our idols. Let's come back to dependence on God alone.

SHABBAT SHALOM

REFLECTION:

WHAT IDOLS DO you need to let go of?

WHAT HOLDS A GRIP OVER YOU, so much so that you worship at its altar and bring sacrifices to it, instead of allowing God to be your one true source?

19. FUEL

But those who wait on the Lord Shall renew their strength; They shall mount up with wings like eagles, They shall run and not be weary, They shall walk and not faint.

— ISAIAH 40:31 (NKJV)

I am generally an optimist. I expect things to work out, one way or another.

So when I am driving and the fuel gage starts to go into the red I know there is still enough left in the tank to take me quite a way. And when I am in a hurry I have a tendency to just assume there will be another petrol station a little further, somewhere...

But sometimes there just isn't. Sometimes that one you passed was your chance. And the amount of times I have limped into the next station on the very last fumes of the tank, nerves shredded - you would think I would learn!

In fact, in the first car I owned I had several instances where the car was literally lurching back and forward, gasping for air, as it were, as I pulled up.

There is a better way. Erm, obviously! And I realise most people know this already when it comes to cars. But how much do we know this when it comes to our lives?

God says one of the purposes for the Sabbath is for us all to be refreshed. And that refreshing is in three different areas, three types of fuel if you like – physical, emotional, and spiritual.

FIRSTLY, we need *physical fuel*. God knows the bodies he has given us. As the stewards of our lives we have a duty to steward our bodies. They are not a prison or our enemies, they are the homes we live in and the vessels that carry us into the purposes he has.

And if God says we need to rest so we can be refreshed, no amount of spiritualising this will change that wisdom. So firstly, let's be practical. *God gives us a break, so sleep, rest, relax.* Even feast a little. It's good for you.

Secondly, we need *emotional fuel.* Our emotions need

a break too. Otherwise we can become too tightly wound.

When I am becoming irritable, find it hard to concentrate, am being less playful with my children – then I know it is time for a break. Not from them (well, occasionally yes haha!), but from stress.

Stress is not the circumstances alone, it is something about my response to them. That is why Jesus said, 'Come to Me all you who are heavy laden, and I will give you rest'.

PETER SAID, '*Give all your worries and cares to God, for he cares about you.*' (1 Peter 5:7 NLT)

You can try to do this every moment of every day, but God is so practical he has scheduled it in our diaries. A block of time where he says we are to *specifically* remember to do this, because the week gets busy and cares mount up without us even realising. He gives us twenty four hours to breathe deeper and let go of anxiety.

Thirdly, we need *spiritual fuel*. We need to find a way to draw off God the strength we need to pursue the life he has given to us.

Now sometimes this is taking time for prayer, reflection, reading the Bible or other books. But sometimes it may be about taking a walk in nature, or with friends somewhere.

God speaks to everyone differently. So know what refreshes you spiritually and do that.

WE LIVE CLOSE to the beach, and often on the Sabbath we will take a walk along the promenade, with no real aim in mind but to relax. And this for me provides physical, emotional, *and* spiritual fuel.

I reconnect with Denise if we haven't had much chance to speak in the week. I throw stones into the sea with Isaac. And all the while God is filling the tank.

God fills the tank in different ways for all of us. Some cars run on petrol, some on diesel, some are hybrid or electric. But whatever the type they all need fuel of *some* sort. Likewise, we may all find energy and get refreshed in different ways, but we all need fuel for the journey.

Neglect our need for fuel in all three areas and we may find ourselves limping, gasping, into God's petrol station, desperate for a refill and nerves shredded. Worse still, we may end up with a breakdown.

God says this is not necessary – there's a station each week, and you can pull in, fill up, and relax before you set off again.

The Sabbath is God's antidote to stress. Don't let the tank get too empty. This Sabbath, let's take full advantage. God fills the tank, but we need to pull in, stop the car, and plug in.

SHABBAT SHALOM

REFLECTION:

IN WHAT WAY is your tank empty?

WHERE ARE you gasping or limping?

IT'S time to be real about the fuel you need in each area, so you can do something about it and ask God to fill the tank.

PRACTICAL:

WHAT FILLS your tank in each of these three areas? What can you do this week to make that a reality?

20. HOLIDAY

'..enjoy the Sabbath and speak of it with delight..'

— ISAIAH 58:13 (NLT)

The Sabbath is a special day, not just a Pitstop. It is important that we understand this. It is a celebration not just a pause for breath between bouts of work.

Think of it like a Summer holiday, once a week.

So it is not a time to get all the tasks done, tempting though that is. Except maybe things that are enjoyable and good for your soul, rather than part of your everyday grind.

One simple way to approach the Sabbath is to ask ourselves what we do when we actually go away for a holiday?

The answer is - *we plan and we prepare*. Some people plan their holidays meticulously, others like to plan them very roughly and explore as they go. But either way, a degree of planning helps ensure that we will have a good time when we are away. We want the time to actually serve its purpose and refresh us rather than being stressful, so we do what we can to make that possible.

Practically that means -

We finish tasks we know will otherwise intrude, **wherever possible. Make those calls, decisions, contacts - whatever we need to do - before we leave.**

WE MAKE sure we have accommodation and travel arranged, so our stay will be comfortable and not a source of stress. We find out a little bit about where we are going. We basically do all we can to ensure that the time away is firstly restful and secondly quality time with the others on the trip.

Likewise, Jewish people enter into a time of preparation before eat Sabbath. They make sure the shopping is done. The household tasks such as cleaning are done. Affairs are in order. Everything is ready to make it *feel* like a holiday.

The truth is if we can treat the Sabbath like a proper

holiday we will enjoy it and benefit far more than if we collapse into it each week and drag ourselves back at the end!

WHEN YOU GO on holiday you expect it to be *different*. That's the key. If you take all your work or study with you it won't feel like much of a holiday. Just different scenery for your work!

You aim to create a holiday atmosphere. You say things like *'Well, we're on holiday...'* as you help yourself to a second (and third) portion of dessert...

You switch off your phone, don't check your e-mails, don't try to pursue business. You try to be present for your family.

With the Sabbath we have to *build* something, individually and as families - that sanctuary or palace in time that Heschel talked about - and part of that means preparing like we would for a holiday where we go away.

Here's an example of what this means practically in my case. I cook Saturday brunch each week, and I used to head out to the bakery each Saturday morning, metaphorical bow and arrow in hand, to bring back fresh bread and other produce from the wild (aka the shops..).

But we started to feel weird about this. It meant I was running around buying stuff and Denise was at home with the boys. So instead we decided to make sure we bought everything we needed on Friday afternoon instead. That way, when the Sabbath comes, there is no rushing, only lolling, playing, eating, and maybe a bit of cooking.

We might even move the cooking to Friday too, although I actually find that relaxing most of the time (except when I enter an imaginary Masterchef competition in my head..).

The Sabbath is a holiday every week and we don't need to pack or unpack!

So LET's treat this Sabbath like a holiday. I mean *really* - treat yourself to a proper holiday. See how it feels! I guarantee it will feel good. Perhaps even a bit naughty at first. But then repeat, each Saturday, however you can, until the Sabbath is no longer some romantic idea or religious ritual. It is an integral part of your week. The holiday part!

SHABBAT SHALOM

REFLECTION:

DO you see the Sabbath as a holiday?

PRACTICAL:

WHAT CAN you do to prepare for the Sabbath more thoroughly?

WHAT WOULD MAKE it feel more like a holiday?

WHAT CAN you do in advance that you normally do on the Sabbath itself?

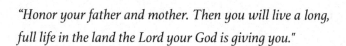

21. FAMILY (2)

"Honor your father and mother. Then you will live a long, full life in the land the Lord your God is giving you."

— EXODUS 20:12 (NLT)

Togetherness is at the heart of the Sabbath, and it starts at home with the family.

Friday night is often a time when families congregate. Everyone has gone their separate ways in the week. On the Sabbath we all come together to reconnect and remind ourselves that this is the bedrock of who we are.

For us as a family there is this sense that however busy the week is, we can look forward to some quality time when the Sabbath comes.

In Jewish culture children who no longer live at home will often come back to their parents for this Friday night meal. It becomes a point of contact and continuity. We acknowledge that our lives are now separate yet we maintain the generational bonds that can so easily go missing.

'Observe the Sabbath day' is the fourth commandment of the ten, the next one is *'honour your father and mother, then you will live a long, full life in the land the Lord your God is giving you'*. These are the only two positive commandments (as opposed to *'do not..'* type prohibitions), and they are put together.

God places both observing the Sabbath and honouring our parents on the same level as not having idols, murdering, coveting, etc. That should cause us to sit up and take notice.

IT IS no coincidence they are together either. For Jewish people they are very often practically entwined. The Sabbath gives us a space to maintain contact, and *both observing the Sabbath and the command to honour your parents come with the benefit of extending and enhancing life.*

In our western, individualistic societies we have often lost the sense of intergenerational families and communities. But in the middle eastern culture of the Bible this is a central theme and principle. Perhaps as a culture we need to re-learn some of this, particularly where loneliness and isolation can be such a blight for older people.

For us, and I am sure many of you, this can often mean phone calls and FaceTime, as distance or practicalities intervene. But it challenges me to consider that God places such a high value on these things. I must learn to also, trusting that the blessings and benefits will follow. God says all this because He is good and wants the best for us and our families.

The Sabbath commandment is the pivot in the ten commandments. The first three are about our relationship with God. The last six are about how we relate to others. And they start with the instruction to honour our father and mother.

IT MAKES sense that the first stop in the list of commands relating to others is to honour those who gave us life and raised us. As a parent there is also a sense of sowing and reaping – how do I want my children to be with me as they grow older and finally leave home?

Even in a broader sense, the Sabbath also reminds us we are not a collection of individuals making our way in the world but a family on a journey together.

So this Sabbath, let's consider our approach to

family. Who do we need to honour? Parents? Others on the journey with us? The Sabbath gives us a moment each week to be intentional about this. And God says as we do, we will find one of the keys to a long and fruitful life.

SHABBAT SHALOM

REFLECTION:

WHAT FAMILY MEMBERS or close friends do you need to keep or build contact with this Sabbath?

HOW CAN you intentionally build this sense of honour and family into your routine, especially on the Sabbath?

22. TIME

> '*So teach us to number our days, That we may gain a heart of wisdom.*'

— PSALM 90:12 (NKJV)

Judaism, says Heschel in *The Sabbath*, is a religion that sanctifies time.

It is remarkable that *the very first thing described as holy in the Bible is the Sabbath*. And nothing is referred to in the ten commandments as holy *except* the Sabbath.

Heschel uses three beautiful terms to describe the Sabbath - A palace in time. A sanctuary in time. A cathedral in time.

As I read the New Testament I don't see Jesus or his disciples contradicting this sense of the holiness of the Sabbath. Rather, in saying it was 'made for man' I see Jesus actually *emphasizing* the role of the Sabbath as a sanctuary and a blessing for us.

And Heschel's phrase – *a cathedral in time* – resonated with me. I think Sabbaths are actually like cathedrals in so many ways -

They are accessible to everyone - they are not exclusive. They do not discriminate based on social class or status, popularity or power.

The invitation to the Sabbath goes out each week to everyone – come as you are. No dress code. Simply come and be refreshed.

IN THIS SENSE the Sabbath is also like the Gospel - *the invitation is sent to everyone and anyone.*

They welcome us - Sabbaths are spaces inviting celebration, reflection, and recalibration. And these are the things that help us to number our days.

They draw us and keep us on track - like spires rising above the landscape of our lives, Sabbaths provide landmarks. They help us to continue moving onward towards our destination. Sabbaths mark time.

They tell stories – the stained glass windows in cathedrals told the stories of the Bible and especially the Gospel. When the light shone through them it illuminated the truth to everyone inside.

The Sabbaths provide a time for the light of God to shine through the windows of our souls, reminding us of the truth and of the new story of our lives.

THEY KEEP *us together* - Sabbaths provide gathering points. They function as community building times.

They help us develop and grow in our relationship with God - because the journey of faith is going deeper into simple truths not spiralling into theological complexity and minutiae.

The Sabbath is a weekly watering hole for the soul. It is fundamentally a simple celebration of what God has done, is doing, and will do in and through us. That is why it is holy.

The Sabbath commandment occupies fully a quarter of the verses of the ten commandments – four out of sixteen. It is, says Heschel, *'the most precious jewel given to us from the treasure house of God'*.

This Sabbath let us relish and revel in this gift, this cathedral in time that God built for us, so we can truly learn to number our days.

SHABBAT SHALOM

REFLECTION:

WHAT ASPECTS of this cathedral analogy resonate with you?

WHAT WOULD you like God to illuminate for you today?

PRAYER:

LORD, please shine the light of your love through windows of my soul. Please help me to enter the space you have provided and find light, illumination, and guidance.

23. SEASON

'For in six days the Lord made the heavens, the earth, the sea, and everything in them; but on the seventh day he rested. That is why the Lord blessed the Sabbath day and set it apart as holy.'

— EXODUS 20:11 (NLT)

'Remember that you were once slaves in Egypt, but the Lord your God brought you out with his strong hand and powerful arm. That is why the Lord your God has commanded you to rest on the Sabbath day.'

— DEUTERONOMY 5:15 (NLT)

As we see in these verses, the main difference between the first and second version of the ten commandments was the reason God gave them for honouring the Sabbath. I believe this actually shows us something very key about both our relationship with God and the purpose of the Sabbath itself.

God gave the children of Israel the first version in Exodus as they emerged from 400 years of slavery in Egypt. They needed to understand their new identity as his covenant people.

HE TOLD them *just as I rested after creation you should too -* you are now mine and you represent me. The shift in identity was so dramatic that God told them to take time to remind themselves of it every week.

The sad truth is that they still failed to enter the promised land because they had not yet grasped this sense of what it meant to be God's people. Cue forty years of wandering in the wilderness, instead of what should have been a short journey. Sound familiar?

How often do you and I also struggle to grasp the truth of who God says we are?

As they were about to finally enter the promised land forty years later God reminded them of his commandments. But he added a new focus for the Sabbath that would help them in the new season.

The only way they could be victorious in the battles ahead was to allow *God* to lead them, to rely on *his* power and not their own. So -

---

HE TOLD them to remember each week how he had rescued them from Egypt, defeating Pharaoh and his armies by his might, not theirs.

AND HOW OFTEN DO WE also struggle to grasp this need to rely on God's strength rather than our own?

God was also preparing them for the season of building to come. He told them to remember what it was like to be slaves, so they could build a different kind of society, where they would always stay compassionate towards the foreigners and other vulnerable people who lived within their communities.

This second time as they entered the promised land there was no grumbling. *The new generation had perhaps finally embraced their identity as God's children.*

I think for all of us it can take a while to catch up with the season we are in. We resist and struggle and often only realise what God is doing after a lot of pain!

But God does know what he is doing, and he wants to speak to us about it. He also knows what comes next in our lives, and he wants to prepare us for it.

———

HE IS SO OFTEN DOING MORE and speaking to us more in the specifics of the season than we realize.

This simple change in the ten commandments shows how *he gave us the Sabbath as a tool to help us keep in step with him in every season.* He cares for us, he is training us, and he wants to help and encourage us in the process.

This Sabbath let's take time to ask God what lessons we need to learn today, so we can flourish and become more fruitful in him.

SHABBAT SHALOM

———

REFLECTION:

WHAT SEASON ARE YOU IN?

WHAT DOES God want to teach you in this season?

. . .

WHAT DOES he want to do in you today to prepare you for the season ahead?

24. EGYPT

'Remember that you were once slaves in Egypt, but the Lord your God brought you out with his strong hand and powerful arm. That is why the Lord your God has commanded you to rest on the Sabbath day.'

— DEUTERONOMY 5:15 (NLT)

As we saw last week, this was the *second* version of the Sabbath commandment, which God gave the children of Israel forty years after the original ten commandments, as they were finally exiting the wilderness and entering the promised land.

God commanded them to stop every week and remember the journey they had been on. Why was this so important? It's because it could teach them so much about both who God was and who they were.

The same principles also apply to our journey with

God. There are four key stages, which we will look at in turn:

Egypt

Wilderness

Promised land

Mountain

Today let's think about *Egypt* -

When the Israelites exited the Red Sea Pharaoh and Egypt no longer had a hold. His men were drowned, his claim and power to hold them gone. *But Egypt still had a grip on their psyche.*

Egypt was slavery, toil, and powerlessness. It was serving a wicked and cruel master whose response to their cries was to make life even harder for them.

The Bible tells us that before salvation we were lost and slaves to sin. But sometimes we forget where we were before we encountered God. We change by increments so we become accustomed to our freedom and can take it for granted.

It's like when other people are astonished how our children have grown, or how different we look when they haven't seen us for a long time. It has been so gradual we can't see the contrast as they do.

God tells us to remember each week what things were really like and just how far we have come.

THE BIBLE TELLS us we overcome by the power of our 'testimony', which really means our story. A key to victory for the Israelites was to remember their story each week. The same is true for us.

It is interesting that they both struggled to obey the Sabbath in the wilderness, and also complained and yearned for Egypt when things became difficult.

It seems so crazy to yearn for a place where you were oppressed slaves. Yet how often are we tempted to return to our Egypts when things get tough?

IT IS dangerous to promise anyone a new life with God without battles or trials, because what God actually promises is to be with us *in* the battles, not to take us on a route with no struggle or enemies. Sometimes when we yearn to go back it's because our concept of the journey was unrealistic.

But how do we fully let go of Egypt? Next week we will look at the wilderness, where God purges us of the *effects* of Egypt. But the first key God gives us is to remember how things *really* were, what it was like to be a slave to sin, and how far we have come. Never romanticise what life was like before!

God says rejoice in your freedom. Remember the

stark contrast between your old life before you met him and now.

Don't dwell on yesterday, last week, or odd occasions when maybe things seemed even a little easier than they are today. Remember instead what the 'miry clay' was really like, and think about what it is like to now have a firm foundation under your feet, to stand on the solid rock, and breathe clean air as a free man or woman!

You're a long way from Egypt. And you are no longer a slave.

SHABBAT SHALOM

———

REFLECTION:

WHAT WAS Egypt (your old life) really like?

WHAT IS life like now in comparison?

WHAT ASPECTS of Egypt are you tempted to return to and why?

25. WILDERNESS

'Don't copy the behaviour and customs of this world, but let God transform you into a new person by changing the way you think.'

— ROMANS 12:2 (NLT)

It is in transformation that we find the greatest blessings of God, but the process is not always easy or comfortable.

When the Red Sea closed behind the children of Israel they were free from Egypt. God took them across the wilderness to the edge of the promised land, where the Jordan river would also part and they would enter.

Yet somehow they ended up stuck in the wilderness for forty years. In fact, that whole generation had to die out before the next one could enter the promised land. And the reason for this -

It took God a short time to get the children of Israel

out of Egypt, but forty years to get Egypt out of the children of Israel.

The people became fearful because they had not embraced what it meant to be God's children and have him fighting on their behalf.

They still saw themselves as grasshoppers rather than conquerors – a negative self-image that was the legacy of their slavery in Egypt.

In stark contrast, forty years later when Joshua led the new generation across the Jordan into the promised land, there was no grumbling or doubt recorded. A new generation had arisen, who had never tasted slavery and had a stronger sense of who they were in God.

How do we apply this to our own lives?

We all have to pass through that transition when we must allow God to purge us of our low self-esteem, our fear of lack – every last hangover from our past life of oppression in Egypt.

IN THE WILDERNESS we start to make the transition into our new creation identity, but it can be painful at times, and painstakingly slow compared to what we would like. True transformation is a process, and if we are honest it can be hard letting go of who we used to be.

But if we want to step into the promised land God

has prepared for us, we *must* go through this. And a great key to how we can negotiate this more quickly is hidden in the story.

It says in Exodus 1:13 (NLT) *'So the Egyptians made the children of Israel serve with rigor'*. Then God repeatedly demanded to Pharoaoh *'Let my people go, that they may serve me in the wilderness'*. And the same Hebrew word, *'abad'*, to serve, is used both cases.

So we must go from serving a cruel, heartless master to understanding what it means to serve as children of a God who loves us. The old identity must be replaced with the new one.

The only way to fully rid ourselves of Egypt is to fully embrace our new identity as children of God.

THE CHILDREN of Israel came back forty years later to the same place they had originally been. I once heard Graham Cooke say this – you don't fail with God, you just get to take the same test over and over again! We all know what it is like to feel like we are 'going round the mountain' in certain areas.

So it may be a struggle today, *but If you let him God will continue to transform you*, as you explore that new creation reality. And the Sabbath is one the best tools he has given us for accelerating the process, a time to remember and embrace our true identity in him, so we each become ready to enter our promised land.

SHABBAT SHALOM

REFLECTION:

IN WHAT WAYS do you feel like you are in the wilderness?

WHAT AREAS of your identity still carry traces of the Egypt mindset and low self-esteem?

WHAT DOES God want to say to you today to make you more ready to enter your promised land?

26. PROMISED LAND

'The people of Israel must keep the Sabbath day by observing it from generation to generation. This is a covenant obligation for all time.'

— EXODUS 31:16 (NLT)

The command to remember the journey from Egypt came as they were just about to enter the promised land. Why did God want them to look back to this event from forty years earlier as they were about to step into their destiny? And why every week, forevermore?

Clearly it was not just about that moment, but about everything that was to come. And it is just as relevant to us today.

The promised land sounds so lovely – a land of milk and honey. But there were giants in the land to defeat. In fact there were enemies all around!

As they stepped into the fulfilment of the promises

and purposes of God, they had to fight *real enemies* for *actual territory.*

It is the same in our lives. As long as we are simply wandering in the wilderness, wrestling for our identity, barely surviving, we face minimal opposition.

This battle for our identity is real of course. The devil knows if he can keep us in a place where we see ourselves and God as small, we will remain in the wilderness.

But God brought them out of Egypt for a purpose, and the same is true for you and me too.

WHEN WE DETERMINE to lay hold of what God has promised and step into the ring to make a difference, then we usually face new opposition. *But the battle and the promise go together!*

And when we start to understand that God has called us to live in the promised land, something comes alive in us.

We realise that if we are designed for the promised land, we are equipped for the battles ahead, anointed to slay giants and take territory as we step into freedom and purpose.

We are also equipped to farm the bees, milk the cows, and work in whatever ways we are called to in order to become fruitful. Paul said God's grace was what allowed him to labour the way he did.

And God says a key to our ongoing success is to each week stop and remember that he has brought us from being slaves into this flourishing, this purposeful living. That was the whole point!

The same God who took us out of our Egypt is the one who will take us into our promised land.

WHAT IS the promised land for you? Is it that job that you know God gave you, but which seems to be a struggle? Is it finding a partner, having children, or flourishing in your finances? A business or creative vision that God has put in your heart? Perhaps it is just beginning to live in freedom and without fear. Whatever it is -

No territory or destiny promised to us by God comes without a struggle. Just like the original promised land the biggest challenges and opposition arise in every God ordained promise coming to fruition in our lives.

So be encouraged - opposition doesn't mean you are on the wrong path. *The battle and the promise go together!*

This Sabbath let's take time to remember that the battle really belongs to him. He rescued us, he is transforming us, and *he is bringing us into fruitful, purposeful lives in the midst of every challenge.*

Let's look to him and draw from him as we boldly step forward!

SHABBAT SHALOM

REFLECTION:

WHAT IS YOUR PROMISED LAND?

WHICH BATTLES DO you need God's help in today?

27. MOUNTAIN

'...and now, here I am this day, eighty-five years old. As yet I am as strong this day as on the day that Moses sent me; just as my strength was then, so now is my strength for war, both for going out and for coming in. Now therefore, give me this mountain of which the Lord spoke in that day;'

— JOSHUA 14:10-12 (NKJV)

Stepping into the life God has for us is like entering the promised land. It is a place of blessings, of challenges, lessons learned in victory and defeat, territory hard won and battle stories we remember.

But God has something further waiting for each of us - a unique purpose, or calling.

Caleb was one of the two spies who brought a good report about the promised land. He was ready to enter, only to be cruelly made to wait for forty years.

Once they finally went in Caleb fought alongside the others. After five years or so, however, he said, *'now give me this mountain that God promised me!'*

For each of us there comes a point when we need to step into God's specific destiny and purpose for our lives.

CALEB BECAME restless just fighting in the general battles – he wanted to fight for the mountain God had promised would be his home.

Sometimes this restlessness can be a product of God trying to focus our strength and attention on the area where we are called to really make a difference and impact others.

I don't know what your mountain is, but God does. If you don't yet know, ask him and he will begin to show you. And don't ignore the nudge when it comes.

He wants to whisper purpose, clarity, and precision into your heart. It is time to point you in the direction of your mountain.

It may be in your family, your workplace, your creativity, or a specific vocation. Whatever it is, God wants to stir that passion in your heart. He tells us to remember the journey each Sabbath so he can build our faith for the destination.

Sometimes he just needs to remind us of a promise

he spoke to us long ago, or a dream he put in us.

Caleb could be bold because he wasn't asking for something new – he was claiming a promise God had already made to him!

Caleb receiving Hebron is actually the very last thing listed in the battles and the allocation of land for each tribe. He was one of the first to receive the promise of specific territory, but seemingly the last to receive it – forty-five years after he had spied out the land, and five years after they had all entered.

It is only after Caleb received his mountain, however, that it says, '*And the land had rest from war*'. Because -

---

God doesn't forget his promises or his purposes, even though it may seem that way to us.

GOD WASN'T content till Caleb had his inheritance, and the same is true for you and me. God will not stop working in and through us, and on our behalf, until we are occupying the very territory he has promised us.

Caleb said, '*my strength for battle is just as it was when I was younger*'. You may feel like you have missed it completely. But God says whatever the hold ups, however fierce the fight has been or is, you are still strong for the battle. And he is still with you, he hasn't given up on you, the promise and the mountain are still there waiting. *The gifts and call of God are without repentance.*

He was with you in every battle so far. He will be with you in this one too, the one that is closest to your heart, the one where the biggest fruitfulness of your life lies.

Caleb knew there were giants remaining in his territory. But he also realised the same God who had been with him all in the previous battles, would be with him in this very personal one.

This Sabbath, remember that God wants to bring you into the true destiny and purpose he has for your life. You've been faithful in the fight so far. It's time to pray and boldly ask, *'now give me my mountain'.*

SHABBAT SHALOM

REFLECTION:

WHAT MOUNTAINS (DOMAINS) *has God promised that you need to fight for?*

WHAT PROMISES DOES *God want to remind you of and how can you pursue those goals today?*

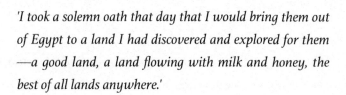

28. SPY

'I took a solemn oath that day that I would bring them out of Egypt to a land I had discovered and explored for them —a good land, a land flowing with milk and honey, the best of all lands anywhere.'

— EZEKIEL 20:6 (NLT)

Now the Lord said to Moses, "Send out men to explore the land of Canaan, the land I am giving to the Israelites."

— NUMBERS 13:1 (NLT)

This is a postscript to our - *Egypt, Wilderness, Promised Land, Mountain* - mini-series. I want to encourage you with this final thought -

God had already discovered and spied out the promised land himself.

When God brought the children of Israel to the edge of Canaan he instructed Moses to send men to spy it out and explore it. As we have seen, only Joshua and Caleb brought a faith filled report, even though they all saw the same abundance in the land.

We'd all like to think we would be like Joshua and Caleb. But before we judge those other spies too harshly, let's consider our own lives - I'm starting with me first -

I think when God gives us a glimpse of the promised land we too can easily let fear, worry, uncertainty, or all manner of insecurities and distractions stop us from pursuing that goal or vision.

When we see the giants we can become despondent or discouraged, even when we know deep down that God has brought us to that place.

But this verse in Ezekiel tells us something extraordinary -

God searched for the promised land and spied it out because he was looking for a future for his people, a destiny that was a perfect, long term fit!

I LOVE how God calls it *'The best of all lands anywhere.'* I know I want the best for my children, and that's exactly how this sounds to me - God wants the best for his children.

When it says that God '*discovered and explored*' the land, it is actually the same Hebrew word - *'tûr'* - as the instructions he gave to the Hebrew spies.

God had literally gone before them and done what he was asking them to do.

God had purposefully spied out and explored every detail. That is why he could confidently tell Moses to send out spies - he just wanted and expected them to agree with him.

The same is true for our lives.

God wants us to see the opportunities ahead the same way he sees them, because he has already spied them out for us.

WHEN THEY WERE STILL captives in exile in Babylon God reassured the children of Israel - *'I know the plans I have for you, says the Lord. Plans to prosper you and not to harm you, to give you a hope and a future.'* Jeremiah 29:11 (NIV)

Even when we feel like a captive to our circumstances God is already searching out a perfect future for us.

When God places a vision in your spirit, he isn't asking whether you can do it. He is showing you a territory he has already discovered and explored for you!

He has seen every giant you're going to come up against, sampled every vineyard and beehive, and made sure it is the perfect fit for you. He just wants you to see it all through his eyes - through the eyes of faith not fear.

So you can embrace the future he has for you with confidence and pursue the dream he has placed in your heart with boldness.

He actually *found it* for you, explored it, and said yup - this is the perfect fit for my son or daughter. This is his or her promised land. Giants, battles, idols, and all!

What dreams have you given up on too easily? It's time to pick them up again and remember - if God promised it to you, if he called you to a territory, then he has already spied it out for you! It is your's for the taking. He's just waiting for you to agree with him and step forward!

SHABBAT SHALOM

REFLECTION:

WHERE DO you need reassurance that God has gone before you?

. . .

WHAT DISCOURAGEMENTS DO CAN you brush off, or promises do you need to pick up again?

WHERE DO you need to start agreeing with God for your future and destiny?

29. DREAMS

When Joseph's brothers saw him coming, they recognized him in the distance. As he approached, they made plans to kill him. "Here comes the dreamer!" they said. "Come on, let's kill him.."

— GENESIS 37: 18,19 (NLT)

It is hard to dream during the week. We have our heads down and we plough on. We get tasks done, we try our best, and we never get to the end of what needs doing, let alone the things we really want to do. It can feel like the familiar tries to kill off all our dreams!

But dreaming is extremely important.

It is interesting how many of the greatest encounters with God in the Bible involved dreams.

Joseph was called a dreamer, and he also interpreted other people's dreams, which saved his whole family plus countless people from the surrounding nations.

The prophet Daniel also interpreted dreams that came from God.

It says that God came to Abraham after he had fallen into a deep sleep, and affirmed his covenant to him.

Jacob dreamed of a ladder ascending to heaven, with angels ascending and descending.

God appeared to Solomon in a dream and told him to ask for whatever he wanted – Solomon asked for discernment and wisdom to govern God's people, and God was pleased with him for this, so he promised to give him what he asked for and also great riches and fame.

Dreaming is good for the soul, especially when we let God get involved with those dreams.

WE READ in Psalm 78:40-42 (NKJV), that God was not pleased with the people of Israel because they limited him through their thinking in the wilderness. Their understanding of what he could do was still too small.

God does not like to be underestimated by his people, even in the wilderness.

Yet how easy is it for us to limit God, in the busyness of our schedules, or when life feels like a wilderness? We place limitations on how much he can bless us, on what we can expect him to do for and through us, of what his plans are for our lives. In short, it is easy for us to think too small, just like the Israelites!

The Sabbath gives us a window to dream with God.

I AM NOT TALKING about just asking God for things, or wealth, or even asking him to fulfil our existing goals. I am talking about lifting the limits off our thinking and allowing God to give us a bigger vision than we can currently imagine.

Often this comes when we are relaxed and simply letting our mind wander and wonder.

When God wanted to give Abraham a bigger vision he took him outside his tent and told him to look up at the night sky.

Each Sabbath is an opportunity to take a moment to step outside the tent of our lives and dream a little bigger with God.

So this Sabbath let's dream! Let's ask God where we have limited him and let go of those limitations. And as he catches us, often off guard, let's recognise the moments when new dreams and visions are being birthed in the incubator of our soul.

There goes that dreamer – this Sabbath let that be you and me!

. . .

SHABBAT SHALOM

REFLECTION:

IN WHAT AREAS is your vision of God's plans and purposes for you smaller than it should be?

WHAT ARE the tents or ways of seeing that God wants to take you out of today, so you can see what he sees?

WHAT DREAMS DOES he want you to dream, or to remind you of?

30. ROOM

'Now after six days Jesus took Peter, James, and John his brother, led them up on a high mountain by themselves;'

— MATTHEW 17:1 (NKJV)

Religion puts a distance between us and God, making us feel unworthy of being in the room with God and party to his thoughts, feelings, and plans.

But Jesus took Peter, James, and John with him up the mountain, where his face shone like the sun and he met with Elijah and Moses to discuss the crucifixion.

He also took them in to the resurrection of Jairus' daughter, and again when he went to pray in anguish at the Garden of Gethsemane.

In the musical Hamilton there's a song called *'The Room where it happens'* in which a character (Aaron Burr) sings about how he wants to be in the room where the big, crunch decisions are made.

I wanna be
I've got to be
In the room where it happens

We are invited to be partners in God's program yet too often we can feel like jellyfish floating on life's currents. Each Sabbath invites us back to God's room and to intimacy.

JESUS SHOWED us what true intimacy with God looks like and what it means to stay in fellowship with his father. He also made a way for us to experience this.

God never wanted to exclude his people from being in the room with him. He walked with Adam in the cool of the day, the implication being one of sharing and fellowship not just instruction.

To become a child of God, forgiven and living as a new creation, means that you and I are invited into 'the room where it happens' - whoever we are, wherever we are.

God reveals his heart and plans to those who are willing to open their own hearts wide to him. This is the key to intimacy. Not perfection, nor strenuous religious activity - just access, openness and a humble heart.

We see it in the life of Abram - God was preparing to destroy Sodom and Gomorrah but said, *Should I not reveal what I am doing to Abram my friend?* Abraham negotiated with God as a friend.

God spoke with Moses face to face. Psalm 103:7 (NKJV) says *He made known His ways to Moses, His acts to the children of Israel.* In other words, Moses knew God more intimately than those who simply saw what he did.

Whenever someone in the Bible drew close to God and gave him access God began to share his plans with that person.

WE SEE it with Jesus and his disciples, and we even see it with the Samaritan woman at the well.

Jesus said his disciples are his friends, including us. And unlike those first disciples when Jesus took them up the mountain, we now have his Spirit actually *living in us*, just as Jesus promised we would.

The Sabbath is a time that reminds us that God wants to walk with us all 'in the cool of the day'.

God wants us as his friends so he can share his heart with us. That why he brought us into the room!

If we are followers of his son, Jesus, then *we have received an open invitation to be in the room where it happens*, with God, sitting, listening, and talking to him, hearing his plans and even discussing them with him.

Let's take full advantage of the invitation as we lean in this Sabbath.

. . .

SHABBAT SHALOM

REFLECTION:

Do you feel like you are included or excluded from the room with Jesus and the father?

WHAT WOULD it feel like to be in that room?

HOW CAN you let go of any striving and open your heart wider to God today?

31. DIFFERENCE

*"You have six days each week for your **ordinary** work, but on the seventh day.."*

— EXODUS 23:12 (NLT)

*"You have six days each week for your **ordinary** work, but on the seventh day you must stop working, even during the seasons of plowing and harvest.*

— EXODUS 34:21 (NLT)

The Sabbath interrupts our plans. It is different, a break in routine. Israel had a promised land to subdue and a kingdom to build, then they had fields to plow and harvest, but still they had to stop and give themselves to this twenty four hours of difference. So must we.

If we see it as catching our breath between bouts of work, or ignore it, we are missing something. It is not just the absence of what you did before but the insertion of a very *different* block of time into our lives.

Routine is a good thing but living our lives on autopilot is not. Without the Sabbath we can be continuously in that autopilot mode.

THE SABBATH DONE PROPERLY interrupts everything. It breaks our train of thought, our internal and external conversations, all our activity, and replaces them all with different ones for twenty-four hours.

The Sabbath actually disengages the autopilot taking us to our destination. It calls us to do loop the loops and fly upside down just for fun. To remember the joy of living and being just for its own sake. To remember the *why* in the midst of the what.

Some people love routine. They are exemplars of self-discipline and self-management. I find I have to constantly work on both to make sure I am as productive as possible.

But whether you are ruthlessly self-disciplined or hopelessly disorganised, we all have a type of routine. The Sabbath calls us to interrupt and set aside that routine.

In businesses, especially innovative ones, it is often when they step back and take time out of the normal routine of building things that the creative magic comes. The magic of new ideas, new directions, products not yet dreamt of.

So too, the interruption of our routines and schedules can be a very good thing for how we creatively approach our lives. During the interruptions we can find new ideas and directions, even solutions we weren't expecting.

I find God often drops ideas into my spirit when I am least expecting, or metaphorically doing those loop the loops. Sometimes I think the Sabbath is God's way of getting us out the way so he can take over!

However disciplined we are I think we must be interruptible and open to God if we want to experience the full beauty of life and the full scope of God's purposes. The Sabbath helps us to develop this.

IT'S CALLED blue sky thinking when you allow all ideas to flow and be considered. But this can only happen when our normal routine is set aside for a moment and we give ourselves space.

So this Sabbath, enjoy your routine being disrupted, even if through gritted teeth at first. Give yourself to the difference, even if it is not your natural preference or personality. You might grow to love it.

After all, God says it's good for your soul...

SHABBAT SHALOM

REFLECTION:

HOW INTERRUPTIBLE ARE you in your life, and how much is the Sabbath a part of that?

HOW ABLE ARE you to give yourself to the difference God is talking about for the Sabbath?

32. FAITH

'What good is it dear brothers and sisters, if you say you have faith, but don't show it by your actions?'

— JAMES 2:14 (NLT)

Stopping on the Sabbath is an act of faith. Each time we stop we are putting our faith in God to work. By it we declare our belief and trust in God as the creator of all things.

The Hebrew word for faith, *'emunah'*, has the same root as the word *'uman'*, which means craftsman or artisan. This is someone who has practised their craft until it has become integral to who they are.

In the Jewish way of thinking that James describes (the way Jesus thought), faith is not just about beliefs but tied to actions. So as we follow God's rhythms of work, Sabbath, and Festivals, they help us to become fruitful and grow into our full potential.

However, it is a bit like going to the gym – if we don't do it at a set time each day or week we'll soon find we haven't done it for weeks and despite our gym membership we're not getting any fitter! It's easy to kid ourselves (I know this from the many gym memberships I have had with little tangible impact on my gym attendance or fitness levels!).

Stopping on the Sabbath is like exercising muscles we don't use much the rest of the week. They are spiritual muscles, but they need developing just as much as our physical muscles.

IF WE DON'T KEEP a regular appointment we may find we grow weak in these areas -

We'll talk about the rest of God but never enter into it.

We'll talk about trusting God but never really live it out.

We'll talk about the importance of our family and closest relationships but never prioritise them.

We'll talk about how tired we feel but never do anything about it.

We'll talk about how God is our everything but live like he's our extra.

Actions matter. Baptism, for instance, is an action, but one we only need to perform once. It symbolises something very important – the death of our old life and resurrection with Christ.

The Sabbath is a weekly *practice*. God asks us to take a step of faith and stop what we are doing.

So Sabbath is not just an idea it is an action. Faith is like a muscle we exercise through repetition. The Sabbath is our gym. God is the trainer who says practice resting and enjoying the fruits of your labour! We must develop this habit so the strength of our trust and our ability to rest can grow.

The key to how we do the Sabbath is simply this – *regularly*. We commit to practice it as an act of faith.

Practice, and build the muscles. It will help you learn to abide in Him. It will help you to become a master craftsman/woman in the area of rest!

IF WE HAVE NOT DEVELOPED those muscles that we need for resting and abiding in the time God has ordained for practice, how can we possibly expect to be strong in this when we get into the actual fight?

As the saying goes, *'It's too late to prepare when you get into the ring'*. If the Sabbath is the gym, then at the start of each week we step, as it were, into the ring.

So this Sabbath let's be hearers and doers! Apart from anything this is a gym where it's fun to practice!

FAITH

.   .   .

SHABBAT SHALOM

REFLECTION:

WHAT STEPS DO *you need to take to exercise your faith more in the way you approach the Sabbath?*

WHAT WILL HELP *you to make a regular commitment to it?*

33. SUCCESS

'You are the salt of the earth...You are the light of the world...'

— MATTHEW 5:13,14 (NLT)

It is easy to feel we have to do something great for God. But trying to do the spectacular is a huge pressure, whereas being yourself is freedom, and the Bible tells us that God has called us to freedom.

It is so easy for us to smuggle old insecurities into the new life we have in God.

We can start off wanting to be fruitful, but easily find ourselves desperate to be *'someone'*, a *'somebody'* in whatever we feel God has called us to do. The Sabbath invites us to let go of this and remember how to simply *'be'*.

God doesn't put this pressure on us to be great in the world's eyes. He simply asks us to shine the light that is in us. He doesn't ask us to achieve but to overflow. King David said, '*My cup runs over*'. For this to happen we must first be full.

God wants us to redefine what we mean by success and greatness, so it aligns with his concept rather than our own.

IT IS SO easy to do the right things for the wrong reasons – for instance, we can serve just to be noticed or for approval. But God wants our actions *and* our motives to align with his. Only then can we find true freedom.

On the Sabbath we have a time to reflect on God's definition of success for our lives, and in the sifting God wants to pull out the weeds of wrong goals and motivation.

It is uncomfortable when God starts to bring these blind spots to the surface, but it is for our benefit he does it, so we will recognise our need and allow him to heal us.

To be light and salt is not to achieve so much as to be. It is not that achievements won't come as we shine. It is that we are not driven by a desperate need for them.

The Sabbath redefines our relationship with success because *for twenty four hours we stop our attempts to get ahead in the world.*

Instead of wondering how great we are becoming (in

the world's eyes), we must reflect on much more profound issues – *what kind of person* am I becoming? Am I becoming more like Jesus? Am I shining the light that God put in me?

What does success look like in your mind? Maybe God wants to help you redefine this, so your definition of success aligns with his.

I FIND the more my definition of success aligns with God's, the more of his love and light I start to feel shining through me, the less pressure I feel to be what the world expects, or anything other than who God has called me to be.

And this realignment is such an important part of stopping and resting.

So this Sabbath let's consider what 'success' means for each of our lives. And what would it feel like to be truly led by that rather than driven by any desperate need?

SHABBAT SHALOM

REFLECTION:

ARE you led by a quest for fruitfulness in God's eyes, or just success in the way the world defines it?

IN WHAT WAYS does your relationship with success need to change so it aligns with God's?

WHAT DOES God's definition of success look like for your life?

34. ORDINARY

'O Lord, do good to those who are good,
Whose hearts are in tune with you'

— PSALM 125:4 (NLT)

The Sabbath is the most important of all the Jewish festivals - the punishment for breaking it was the most severe.

At first glance this is surprising since it is weekly, and therefore seemingly more mundane than the annual festivals. Yet I think this tells us something very important about God.

The Sabbath isn't tied to a season, harvest, or any one event, as many of the festivals are. The very *reason* it is the holiest festival is because it happens each week and is about recognising God in the midst of our normal routine.

The Sabbath relates to every aspect of our lives and speaks to the very core of who we are.

Since God describes his people as *holy* this means that we are completely set apart for his use. God is interested in our twenty-four hour existence, not just the bits we think of as spiritual.

God wants us to find him in the everyday rhythms of our lives.

A DRAMATIC MOMENT or encounter can grab our attention, and maybe alter the trajectory of our lives in radical ways. And I am not knocking the importance or power of this. Indeed, that was how I came to faith.

But *God wants the encounters we do have to lead to genuine lasting change, so our hearts beat in tune with his.* And the Sabbath is a gift he has given to help us experience this, a drum beat for every week.

So often in looking for God in the spectacular we miss him in the mundane. God is not just looking for a highlights reel.

Paul had an incredible encounter with Jesus – he fell to the ground in a light that temporarily blinded him, the audible voice of God speaking to him - it doesn't get much more dramatic than that!

Yet Paul then spent three years in Arabia and

Damascus, allowing his whole life to be moulded and changed. Just like the first apostles and all of us he had to be trained and transformed. It's easy to forget this when we read about all the amazing adventures he had later.

God's aim has always been to develop a people who *live wholeheartedly in step with him.*

The pinnacle of creation in Genesis was not more and more complexity but a simple heart to heart relationship in a garden between God and people.

JUST AS HEALTH is better than healing, so a lifestyle in communion with God must be our goal, rather than repeatedly lurching from self-sufficiency to dramatic rescue, no prayer to parachute prayer.

The 'Lord's prayer' is about acknowledging God as our source and inviting him into every aspect of our lives, not looking for a spiritual escape hatch.

It is in this spirit that Paul said *'pray without ceasing'* - not a withdrawal from life towards God, but rather fully inviting God into everything we do.

The Sabbath is a key plank of this, sitting as it does at the end/beginning of each week. It teaches and reminds us to attune our hearts to his. It may seem unspectacular but -

It is out of this alignment with God that the river of peace and blessing flows, but also miracles, rescue for others and influence for God.

When you live like this it doesn't matter if you can't get to the right meeting, be at the perfect conference, or hear the ultimate sermon. Because *you and I already have access to the very greatest source of life and love in our everyday lives.* The Sabbath helps us stay connected.

So this Sabbath let's determine to bring the very ordinariness of our lives to God. To invite him into the rhythm of our everyday lives and step into alignment with his heart.

SHABBAT SHALOM

———

REFLECTION:

WHAT AREAS of your ordinary life do you need to invite God into?

IN WHAT WAYS do you need to tune your heart to his today?

35. SIMPLE

So Naaman went with his horses and chariots and waited at the door of Elisha's house. But Elisha sent a messenger out to him with this message: "Go and wash yourself seven times in the Jordan River. Then your skin will be restored, and you will be healed of your leprosy."

— 2 KINGS 5:9,10 (NLT)

It can be hard to keep up with this intense and fast paced modern world, where even the accepted 'truth' seems to change daily, and our lives often feel so full of complexity and ambivalence.

The Sabbath calls us back to simplicity, and I think we need this more than ever before.

The theme of simplicity runs through the teaching of Jesus, and the arguments he had with the Pharisees about the Sabbath revolved around this. Keep it simple -

it's a time for resting, for being refreshed and for healing.

Jesus repeatedly told his listeners not to undermine God's blessings by adding unnecessary man-made rules and rituals.

WE SEE a powerful picture of simplicity in the healing of Naaman, the commander of the Syrian army and also a leper, in the time of the prophet Elisha.

A prompt from a captured servant girl led Naaman to be in Israel, looking for his healing. He brought with him a huge, impressive array of gifts - silver, gold, and ten sets of clothes.

When he went to Elisha's house Naaman became frustrated and angry that the prophet didn't come out himself and dramatically heal him. Fortunately, Naaman's servant persuaded him to stop throwing a tantrum and obey the simple instructions Elisha had issued through his servant.

After he simply dipped in the waters of the River Jordan seven times he was totally healed.

We too can fixate on meeting the right people or wanting God to move in specific ways. We want him to personally appear to us and, as Naaman did, *'wave his hand over the leprosy'* in our lives.

But God has given us a simple instruction - *come back to me each week and wash in the waters of my spirit and my love*. It may not look like much, it may seem too easy or simple. But if we do it, it really will help us to be healed, grow healthier, and find rest for our souls.

Elisha refused payment despite the lavish gifts offered. As Samuel told Saul, *obedience is better than sacrifice*. God's solution to our healing and transformation is a free gift that requires our humility and obedience, not our payment or striving. This is true of salvation and also of the Sabbath.

We can so often miss God in the simplicity of his instructions. We can be looking to others instead of him, or seeking complex answers to our seemingly complex problems.

BUT GOD'S solution is different, and the way to our wholeness is simple obedience not intricate rituals or powerful connections. As Jesus said, we need childlike faith.

Naaman had to wash seven times, and seven in the Bible is the number of perfection, as well as the Sabbath itself.

But this also reminds me of Peter's question to Jesus about whether his disciples needed to be willing to forgive up to seven times - '*Seven times seventy*' was Jesus' answer. In other words, *forgive and keep on forgiving.*

Likewise,I think the answer to how we are cleansed is to wash and keep on washing. We are both saved and being saved. Re-born and being transformed. Wash, rinse, repeat.

Jesus didn't give us detailed new religious instructions. He called us to simplicity in that which was already given. He told us to rest and wash in the waters of God's love, displaying the same humility as Naaman eventually did.

Let's accept he Sabbath's gift of simplicity this week.

SHABBAT SHALOM

REFLECTION:

WHERE HAVE you made things more complex than they need to be?

IN WHAT WAYS can you come back to simplicity?

WHERE DO you need to wash your soul in the waters of God's love and be cleansed?

36. ANTIDOTE

'You have six days each week for your ordinary work, but
on the seventh day you must stop working, even during
the seasons of ploughing and harvest.'

— EXODUS 34:21 (NLT)

Anxiety is a scourge of the modern world - statistics
actually suggest that around a third of us will
experience an anxiety disorder at some point, as defined
medically. A sizeable proportion will take medication to
counter the symptoms.

Anxiety attacks, but God gave his people a special
weapon for the battle against anxiety, an antidote to the
poison of stress - *the Sabbath*.

If the Israelites were ever going to be anxious it was
surely in the seasons of ploughing and harvest - they
depended on the seeds they sowed and the grain they
could harvest to sustain them for the rest of the year. Yet

God specifically commanded them to observe the Sabbath throughout these seasons.

Those fields sat there, bursting with crops, temptingly ripe for the taking. Perhaps the Israelites might have thought they should work for four straight weeks and then take a week off at the end?

Instead, God goes one better. He says - *yes, take that week off* (it's called the festival of shelters or 'Sukkot', and it began after they had harvested all the produce of the land). *But take the Sabbath every week too.*

God says in the midst of your busiest season you must continue to observe the Sabbath rest! Stop, and take a stand against the anxious activity of preparing and stockpiling that seems so necessary. In fact -

---

The busier we are the more important it is for us to rest, the more we need the Sabbath antidote to the poison of anxiety and stress.

WE SEE a precursor of this with the manna - God told the children of Israel not to gather food on the Sabbath, instead he gave a double portion the day before. Yet some could not resist the temptation to look.

They had enough already, but they felt like they needed to get more (though in fact there was none there). And how much does that describe our lives today?

Unlike the manna, however, those fields *did* sit waiting. But God says, *nonetheless stop and take a breather. Be refreshed, connect to me and to each other. And only then go back to it.*

Anxiety and stress can have many causes. But the sense of rest, calm, and peace that the Sabbath contributes to our lives can be a massive help in countering them.

It is liberating to stop mid-harvest, mid-ploughing, mid-problem or circumstance, and say - Father, I choose to give this back and rest in you. I refuse to be anxious about it.

WE SURVEY the fields and we remember the one who made them and created the seasons. We laugh with him and our fellow labourers. We enjoy the fruits of our labour from the previous week and tell stories. We learn and grow.

And then, once refreshed and re-gathered, we get back to it the next day.

Our anxious thoughts can overwhelm us but this Sabbath, if you are feeling anxious, I want you to take a moment, a minute, even an hour if you can. Put every problem or situation or relationship issue into a field in your mind.

Now stand back. Cross the path by the side of the field and survey it all with Jesus by your side. Hand it back to him -

You are his and the field is too, with all its unruly weeds mixed in amongst the good crops.

It will be the same when you come back to it. But you will be different and God will be closer. So this Sabbath let's try to take a break from anxious living.

SHABBAT SHALOM

REFLECTION:

WHEN DO you feel most anxious?

WHAT ANXIOUS THOUGHTS do you find yourself thinking regularly?

HOW CAN you give your anxious thoughts and feelings to God more so he can give you peace?

37. LOVE GOD

Jesus replied: " 'Love the Lord your God with all your heart and with all your soul and with all your mind.' This is the first and greatest commandment. And the second is like it: 'Love your neighbour as yourself.' All the Law and the Prophets hang on these two commandments."

— MATTHEW 22:37-40 (NIV)

The Sabbath contains every aspect of this love Jesus was talking about - to love God, self, and others. Let's consider how it helps us to love God this week.

The fourth (Sabbath) commandment is actually the bridge in the ten commandments between the first three, which deal with our relationship with God, and the last six, which relate to others.

God commanded the Israelites not to make a 'graven' image of him. Yet how easy is it for us to cast

God in the image of our own ideas and wants, rather than get to know him as he really is?

The lower the level of relationship with God, the more dangerous this can become. People have fought unjust wars to satisfy an image of God that had no relation to who he really is, and all in the name of love. But -

---

To love is to know and be known. It is to place the needs of the other equal to or above our own. God wants us to know and love him in this way, just as he loves us.

THE HEBREW WORD FOR LOVE, *ahava,* encompasses many different types of love. The Gospel writers use the word *agape* in their version. *Agape* is the love that meets the needs of others, a love that gives unselfishly.

So if we want to learn to love God, we should ask ourselves - what are his needs? Here are some key ones -

God needs relationship

God is love. He created us as the object of his love, so he needs us to receive this love.

It is a painful thing to love without response. We often talk about the unconditional love of God but unconditional and *unrequited* are two different things. *God desires our response.*

Fellowship is two way. He wants to experience our

response and to be recognised for who he is, not who we create him to be for our purposes.

God needs interaction and conversation

If he created Adam so he could walk and talk with him in the cool of the day, then to love God is to give him real relationship. We see this with Abraham, who God calls his friend.

This means an informal openness of the kind we have with our closest friends. It isn't just functional or transactional. At root it is about both knowing and being known.

The commandment talks about loving God with all of our heart, soul, and mind. This means involving God in every aspect of our lives.

Loving God like this is a far cry from a religious observance or a set of rituals. It is a heart to heart experience, and a sharing of thoughts and plans.

THE DECISION TO be open is up to us, but I believe this is what it means to truly love God. When our obedience comes out of this place it is beautiful, but no amount of grudging or legalistic obedience will create this. God desires relationship, not ticks on a list.

Love is expressed in vulnerability, willingness to share not withholding thoughts or feelings.

Love is warm and vibrant and full of life, it is not cold and dutiful or subservient.

Love is about embracing the other and allowing ourselves to be embraced. It is giving and receiving. This is how we love God.

The Sabbath gives us a space to practice what it means to love God and to put him first. It expresses our delight in him, and his in us.

The heart of the Sabbath is less what we should and shouldn't do, more about a space to nurture our love of God, self, and others.

This Sabbath let's give God space. Let's invite him to love us and let's love him in response by acknowledging him for who he is and giving him room in our lives.

SHABBAT SHALOM

REFLECTION:

Is your relationship with God one of intimacy, or more distant and functional?

How CAN you make a little more space to develop this heart-to-heart relationship?

38. LOVE YOURSELF

Jesus replied: "'Love the Lord your God with all your heart and with all your soul and with all your mind.' This is the first and greatest commandment. And the second is like it: 'Love your neighbour as yourself.' All the Law and the Prophets hang on these two commandments."

— MATTHEW 22:37-40 (NIV)

Love of self is a much misunderstood subject. We are commanded to love others *as we love ourselves*, yet we are also commanded not to love our lives, and to die to ourselves.

We are told not to love this world and yet so much of our self-identity is tied up in the things of this world.

How do we negotiate these and other seemingly irreconcilable pulls on our emotions?

As a pastor and social worker, and working often with groups of men and women around emotional wholeness, I have found this area to be one of the most confused yet vital areas of a healthy life.

Most of us carry around negative messages about ourselves that we have internalised from our past experiences. These have no foundation in the way God calls us to live and love, but are an expression of the brokenness God wants to mend.

The fact we do not love ourselves is not down to some godly motive, it is because we do not think we are lovable or loved. We do not love ourselves because we have not experienced the healing love of God in so many areas of our lives.

The confusion often comes because we feel that to love ourselves means to put our needs above all else, to be selfish, and to ignore the needs of others. This could not be further from the truth.

In reality learning to love ourselves simply means learning to treat ourselves as God wants to treat us.

IT MEANS NURTURING the gifts we have been given, for the benefit of others. It means giving ourselves freedom to explore opportunities and to become who we were created to be.

It means to not dismiss, ignore, or condemn the broken parts of ourselves that need mending, but to invite the necessary healing, so that once fixed these areas of our hearts can better serve the purposes for which they and we were created.

Loving ourselves is not pampering ourselves to the exclusion of all else, it is stewarding and nurturing our hearts and our minds so that all we have is healthy.

When we love ourselves this way we are able to offer the world the best gift we can – a fully present, fully functional version of ourselves.

OTHERWISE WE SPEND our lives trying to use the things of this world and other people to fix or compensate for the broken areas, and bolster our sense of self. Or we just try to avoid them altogether. And either way most of the time we aren't aware that that is what we are doing.

Our wholeness, as we learn to love ourselves, is the very thing that allows us to focus less on our needs and more on serving God and others.

This is what it means to *'love others as we love ourselves'* - our relationship with God teaches us how to love, and changes how we see ourselves.

Understanding what it means to no longer be broken or rejected but instead loved and celebrated, we are then able to bring that gift to others.

The Sabbath is a lesson in loving ourselves. We are

commanded to rest, given a space to be at peace and pull back from striving, or even measuring our progress.

We are called to nurture and learn to love ourselves so that we can better love others.

This Sabbath, let's really take this to heart and put away any notions that loving ourselves is an indulgence. It is part of the building blocks of God community, his kingdom coming to earth.

To hate ourselves is not godly, but to choose to love others because we are so full of love is.

SHABBAT SHALOM

REFLECTION:

HOW MUCH DO you love yourself the way God commands?

IN WHAT AREAS do you need to experience God's love and healing in the way you see yourself?

PRAYER:

FATHER, teach me to love myself the way that you do so I can be whole and learn to love others the way that you do!

39. LOVE OTHERS

'But a Samaritan, as he travelled, came where the man was; and when he saw him, he took pity on him. He went to him and bandaged his wounds, pouring on oil and wine. Then he put the man on his own donkey, brought him to an inn and took care of him.'

— LUKE 10:33-34 (NLT)

Jesus summed up the Torah by those two commandments, 'Love God with all your heart and soul and strength', and 'love your neighbour as yourself'.

He then told this parable in response to the question, 'Who is my neighbour?' The agenda behind the question, however, was really 'Who can I exclude?'

The story teaches us something about how God wants us to love others - both *how* to love and *who* to love.

There are parallels with the Sabbath commandment. God says that everyone should have the same rest, but he doesn't just leave it there. He specifically lists *children, livestock, servants, and any foreigners living amongst you.*

Clearly, he felt there was a danger that these groups would be overlooked. They are all more vulnerable and less powerful, just like that wounded man on the road.

In the busyness of life it is so easy to rush past others, especially those who we may take for granted, or who are easier to overlook.

I THINK the challenge of loving others is so often as much about time as anything else. Firstly, it takes time to recognise the needs of those around us. Secondly, even where we have the intention, we often struggle to *make* the time.

Jesus first mentions a priest and a Levite who don't stop. I think just like them it is easy for us to be so busy with what we consider religious activity or routine that we miss the simple acts of love God places before us each day. This parable makes it very clear what God's priorities are.

As John Mark Comer says in his book, The Ruthless

Elimination of Hurry, *'hurry and love are incompatible'*. Any parent knows this. Anyone who has experienced true friendship or been confronted with someone close to them in a period of crisis knows this too.

In those times we all want to experience the unhurried love of those closest to us. We want them to stop, bandage our wounds, and take time out of their schedule to attend to our needs. Yet are we willing to love others in this way?

Sometimes the most valuable aspect of loving others is just to stop and take time.

THERE'S something else - the parable of the good Samaritan was more remarkable to the Jews listening because the Samaritans were actually not just foreigners but also *enemies* of the Jewish people at the time. Jewish people considered it would make them ritually unclean to mix with a Samaritan.

And Jesus also tells a story not of a Jewish person stopping for a Samaritan, but the other way around! So the Jewish audience are cast in the role of the vulnerable, weaker ones needing care at the hands of their enemies.

The hidden truth in this parable is that Jesus is also teaching us something about how he loves us.

We were all enemies of God, wounded at the side of the road, half-dead, and he stopped for us. He paid the price for us to be forgiven and healed. And he commands us to love others in the same way.

The kind of love Jesus is talking about is *'agape'*. It is more about choosing to meet the needs of others - just as the Samaritan man did in the story - than a warm fuzzy Hollywood feeling.

The Sabbath is one of the greatest weapons God has given us for loving others. It offers us a gift of time, a space to act intentionally. A chance to stop for others, starting with those closest to us.

So this Sabbath, let's not just pass by the needs of those around us. Our children, friends, those in need, however different from us.

This Sabbath, let's decide to love others and let's practice by stopping.

Shabbat shalom

———

Reflection:

In what ways does hurry stop you from loving those around you?

. . .

Who is on the side of the road before you that you might normally pass by?

40. COVENANT

Tell the people of Israel: 'Be careful to keep my Sabbath day, for the Sabbath is a sign of the covenant between me and you from generation to generation. It is given so you may know that I am the Lord, who makes you holy.'

— EXODUS 31:13 (NLT)

God tells us that the Sabbath is supposed to help us remember and reaffirm the covenant we have with him and by extension one another. But what *is* covenant?

The Hebrew word for covenant is *'berit'*, which literally means to cut. Blood represents life in the Bible, so sharing blood means sharing life.

A covenant relationship is therefore a commitment that isn't based on convenience or circumstance, but rather on an unbreakable decision and commitment. It means our lives belong to each other.

This is great news because it means that God's

commitment to us isn't based on our performance. He has bound himself to share his life with all who are willing to enter into that covenant relationship with him.

Covenant means God will not withhold his love nor shut off our access to it because we have made mistakes or even walked away from him. His commitment remains, his grace is always available to us if we are willing to receive it.

MARRIAGE IS the form of covenant relationship we are most familiar with. The rings we wear represent the cutting of the finger to draw blood, just as our covenant with Jesus was sealed with his blood.

When we get married we don't so much join an institution called marriage as make a commitment, a vow, to share our lives with one another through every circumstance. It is more than a legal decision, it is a decision to become one in every way possible. Likewise -

To be in covenant with God means to be one with him, through every season, for better or worse. We may be fallible and fickle, but God is constant and unwavering in his commitment to us.

Notice God offers this covenant on the basis of his shed blood alone. *His commitment does not waver based on our imperfect responses to his love.*

It is in the context of covenant that we learn the lessons of true love. The primary purpose of marriage is the flourishing of love and fruitfulness within that security, of spouses and children.

In the same way, our covenant with God brings us into a form of relationship where there is security and where intimacy can grow. This is far from the idea of a cold, legalistic religion where we try our hardest to please a distant or stern God who is rating our form each day.

Instead, Jesus tells us *I will never leave or forsake you.* God told the children of Israel *I will make with you an everlasting covenant.* Covenant is an expression of a deep passionate commitment and sharing.

Since we are joined by covenant to God, we are also joined by covenant to one another. This means that we must be passionately committed to one another.

OUR GOAL CANNOT BE to get to the top of a pile, but to serve and love others, enhancing the life of our communities.

It is scary for us to imagine that degree of interconnectedness, that level of accountability towards God and others, and alien to our Western mindset. Yet this is exactly what we are called to, and God is radically unapologetic about this.

He does not ask for our opinion about it. He simply proclaims that he will build his people, as living stones, into a single unified, interconnected super-organism. He expects us to operate from a mindset of covenant with one another, just as he does with us.

The more we can understand this idea of covenant, the more we will begin to see how it provides the perfect framework for the adventures God has in store for us.

The Sabbath is a time to remember and reaffirm the covenant that we have with God and one another. So this Sabbath let's remind ourselves that we are a covenant people joined to a covenant keeping God.

SHABBAT SHALOM

REFLECTION:

WHAT DOES covenant mean to you, especially in terms of God's covenant with you?

WHO ARE you connected to in this way?

41. REMEMBER

Remember that you were once slaves in Egypt, but the Lord your God brought you out with his strong hand and powerful arm. That is why the Lord your God has commanded you to rest on the Sabbath day.

— DEUTERONOMY 5:15 (NLT)

The Hebrew word translated remember is *zachor*, and Moses uses it fifteen times in the book of Deuteronomy, which is essentially one long speech that he gave as the children of Israel were about to enter the promised land.

Poverty in the desert caused them to look back at Egypt through rose-tinted spectacles. But affluence in the promised land carried a different danger - *forgetting*.

God wants us to have '*best of all lands*' and to live gloriously off its produce. We are blessed to be a blessing.

But God also knows us. He knows that when things are good and the harvests are plentiful we can easily come to rely on our own efforts and imagine we no longer need him at all.

Before we know it, we are basing all our decisions on the need to acquire more by working harder, getting ahead, and being better than those around us. We lose touch with the source of our blessings so easily.

So Moses says 'remember to remember'. He outlines the details as they are about to enter the bountiful land, and just like God's original command, he links this remembering with the Sabbath.

ONLY ONCE DOES he ask *God* to remember, as a plea rather than a prompt. All the other times he is instructing the people. It is really us who need to remember, not God.

As David said, *praise the Lord and forget not all his benefits.*

The result of not remembering is that we swing from one extreme to another in a never-ending cycle - in poverty we seek God desperately until eventually in his compassion he moves and we are restored. Then, in the light of God's favour we start to forget him, and there is a lag as we ride on the wave of his blessings.

Eventually the wheels start to come off and we return to our knees, desperate once again. And as a loving father God picks us up again, and so the cycle continues.

The Sabbath offers us a way out, a solution to this swinging between desperation and blessing. Remembering helps us to stay steady as we plough our course through the waves of life.

IF WE USE the Sabbath to remember who we are and *whose* we are, then we can escape from the cycle of relief and of despair.

We remember that God is our source, however busy or successful we have been that week with the means of production, and we reset our compass before the next week's activity.

Moses commanded them - *'Remember the Lord your God. He is the one who gives you the power to be successful, in order to fulfil the covenant he confirmed to your ancestors with an oath'* (Deuteronomy 8:18 NLT)

As we too do this we can move away from the frustration of the pendulum swing and enter a steadily growing abundance of heart, from which the blessed life starts to flow.

The children of Israel experienced this swing in the

form of a familiar pattern - prosperity, forgetting, exile, return, prosperity, forgetting, exile, return...

In the midst of this God repeatedly said - *you are not observing my Sabbaths!* You have forgotten to remember! This is what is causing the pattern – *you have lost the rhythm of remembering.*

We must learn from their example and step into a steady flow of God's blessings for our lives.

So this Sabbath let's *remember to remember* - God is always our source and treasure, and this is our only certainty.

SHABBAT SHALOM

REFLECTION:

WHAT DO you need to remember about God and his blessings this week?

WHAT WILL HELP you use the Sabbath to help you remember more?

42. PILGRIMS

'All these people died still believing what God had promised them. They did not receive what was promised, but they saw it all from a distance and welcomed it. They agreed that they were foreigners and nomads here on earth. Obviously people who say such things are looking forward to a country they can call their own. If they had longed for the country they came from, they could have gone back. But they were looking for a better place, a heavenly homeland. That is why God is not ashamed to be called their God, for he has prepared a city for them.'

— HEBREWS 11:13-16 (NLT)

You and I are *pilgrims*, the word that the NKJV translation uses instead of *nomads* above. Pilgrimage seems like an old-fashioned term. It makes us think of cathedrals and monks and people doing penance to afflict their souls.

But it is also a beautiful word because it speaks of a yearning that each of us can identify - that yearning to be truly, fully in union with God. The quest that engulfs us the more we know the one who saved us.

The Sabbath is our destination each week. It brings a completion as the reward of our labours. But also -

---

The Sabbath is a weekly reminder that we are on a journey – the rabbis actually liken the Sabbath to a taste of the kingdom which is to come.

JUST AS ABRAHAM looked to the kingdom beyond where he was, so we look to a glorious future of eternal union with God. The passage above tells us that it pleases God for us to live in this way, as pilgrims.

There are so many destinations that we seek in life. A promotion, a partner, a house, a vocation. These are all good, but the Bible tells us we must keep in mind the ultimate destination for which we are bound.

The Sabbath takes pressure off us because it reminds us that in this life we do not have to arrive at our permanent destination. We are released from the feeling of the donkey straining for that dangling carrot.

I once climbed up a mountain and I found that each time I thought I was arriving at the summit it turned out to just be another crest. Yet when I got up high and finally turned to look back from one of these crests, the view was breath-taking and I could see how far I had come.

Life can be very draining and depressing if we repeatedly feel like we are about to arrive, only to find we are still faced with another climb.

But if we realise that each crest just means a clearer, better view, and a step closer to where we are really heading, then we will be enthused and encouraged for the climb ahead.

The Sabbath is a moment to turn and enjoy the view from whatever spot you have reached.

Knowing there will always be challenges to face and slopes to navigate on route to our ultimate destination, we can enjoy the climb for what it is. We are still travelling.

We look to that kingdom, that union with God for which we were created and into which we are growing every day. This keeps us on the journey and reminds us that we are pilgrims.

EACH SABBATH we let go of other destinations that we have been seeking in the week, that have consumed us. We come back to the place of being pilgrims.

Even as we rest we remember the true journey that

we are on and what really matters. And strangely this yearning in the midst of everything else, provides us with a hidden track that brings peace to our otherwise restless souls.

We are pilgrims on a journey with God, a journey to God, a journey in God.

Pilgrims travel together to make the journey safer, to encourage one another and to seek shelter on the way.

This Sabbath find your fellow pilgrims and rest with them. Remember the journey you are on together and find joy and peace in what really matters.

SHABBAT SHALOM

REFLECTION:

WHERE ARE you in your pilgrimage?

WHO ARE YOUR FELLOW PILGRIMS?

43. RHYTHM

"You have six days each week for your ordinary work, but the seventh day is a Sabbath day of complete rest, an official day for holy assembly. It is the Lord's Sabbath day, and it must be observed wherever you live. In addition to the Sabbath, these are the Lord's appointed festivals, the official days for holy assembly that are to be celebrated at their proper times each year."

— LEVITICUS 23:3,4 (NLT)

I am a work hard play hard kind of guy. But finding the rhythm of life is about more than simply seasons of work followed by seasons of play.

God gave us a template to help us. He is our example for the rest of the Sabbath, and also for the work of the six days.

God's festivals and the Sabbath all function as a pattern of life to help us work hard and play hard.

For instance, the harvest festival comes after the intense labour of the harvest. Passover and Shavuot correspond to the season of sowing and the labour of ploughing.

The Sabbath gives us space to relax each week. Healing is good but health is better. Rescue is good but a steady path is more effective.

A beautiful moment is good but a beautiful rhythm is better.

IT IS natural for there to be different seasons in life and in our spiritual journey. But I have found it is too easy to get trapped in a pendulum swing between a healthy spiritual life and its polar opposite – distance, confusion, and the feeling of being drained.

Jewish life is notable for the consistent disciplined sense of routine that it provides and a basic building block of all of this, along with some common prayers and liturgy, is the Sabbath.

In music the kick-drum (the deepest sounding drum, played with the foot) is the key to creating rhythm. All the other drums play more and work around it, but *the kick is the anchor, setting the beat.*

The Sabbath is God's kick-drum for our lives.

The one consistent feature in the rhythm of our lives

and the landscape of our activity is this pause, this drumbeat keeping us at the right pace for the marathon of life.

Without that we can get so caught up in all the other sounds, the crashing cymbals and busy tom drums, other instruments, etc, that we lose track of the rhythm.

When I succumb to a sense of panic and pressure in any area of my life I find I lose my centre and my sense of peace in God. But -

———

The Sabbath brings us back to that centre and reminds us of the pace God has ordained for our lives.

———

RHYTHM IS important in every area of life not just music. A marathon runner for instance finds a pace that feels comfortable in the long haul and allows them to finish the race strong.

The festivals of God, starting with the Sabbath, do the same for our lives. We need holidays and celebrations. We need to keep in step with the Holy Spirit, for he has helped millions run the race set before us many times over and he knows what it takes to finish.

So this Sabbath let's check the rhythm of our lives.

A solid, enjoyable rhythm is what makes a track feel comfortable, both in musical and athletic terms. The

Sabbath is a drum beat that helps hold the rhythm of life together.

SHABBAT SHALOM

REFLECTION:

HOW MUCH DO you allow God's drumbeat to help you keep a steady rhythm in your life?

WHERE ARE you running too fast or out of sync with the Holy Spirit, and need to return?

44. ENVIRONMENT

Six years you shall sow your land and gather in its produce, but the seventh year you shall let it rest and lie fallow, that the poor of your people may eat; and what they leave, the beasts of the field may eat. In like manner you shall do with your vineyard and your olive grove.

— EXODUS 23:10-12 (NKJV)

Then at last the land will enjoy its neglected Sabbath years as it lies desolate while you are in exile in the land of your enemies. Then the land will finally rest and enjoy the Sabbaths it missed. As long as the land lies in ruins, it will enjoy the rest you never allowed it to take every seventh year while you lived in it.

— LEVITICUS 26:34,35 (NLT)

The land rests every seventh year

> *The beasts of burden rest every seventh day*

> *The wild animals can eat and reclaim the produce of the land*

> *Man lives in harmony with nature*

Rather than just constant use there is a sense of rhythm, stewardship, and responsibility.

The Sabbath is part of a whole system of looking after people, livestock, animals, and the environment. It is an explicit acknowledgment of the links between all these, an environmentalism before it was called that.

It is not some extreme or alternative position to suggest that looking after the home we live in and guaranteeing its future for our children is a good idea. It is biblical, and specifically sabbatical. What is better for the environment is better for the people who live in it.

Mankind's first call was to tend a garden.

WE SEE at one point that God says *the land will be desolate because of their actions* – God actually links the immoral actions of people with the desolation of the land.

When Israel was exiled God only allowed them to return after the land had been repaid all its

Sabbaths. They may have thought their neglect was trivial, God clearly did not! Guess he cares about how we treat his creation.

Equally, we see that wherever the people lived according to God's principles the land flourished and was fruitful. But it was the fruitfulness of harmony not the results of rapaciousness and destruction.

We are stewards of all we have - relationships, children, finances, land, everything. Our enjoyment of all these things runs alongside our responsibility to manage them well.

God continues to call the territory of Israel *his* land, for instance, despite making a covenant to give it to the Israelites. Because *just like us they are stewards only, however much milk and honey is there for the taking.*

The earth is the Lord's and the fullness thereof. How would you want someone to look after *your* land?

We must steward his earth well to be faithful servants. When we give it back God surely won't be impressed with us for handing over a barren, flogged wasteland that we have sucked dry of life.

When it comes to the environment, being faithful simply means leaving the world a better place for future generations rather than destroying it for our own profit and leaving them to pay the price.

THIS IS NOT a political but a Biblical stance, and I am not sure we can conclude differently from reading the words of Jesus, Moses, and all the prophets and other writers of the Bible.

It is interesting that Israel, with this legacy of the Torah, is one of the only nations in the world that entered the 21st century with more trees than it had a hundred years previously. The Jewish National Fund has planted some 240 million trees.

We find this idea of stewardship - of respect, partnership, and harmony with the environment – embedded in the Torah commands and specifically the ones relating to the Sabbath.

This is part of what we looked at earlier - *Tikkun Olam*, or repairing the world. We cannot do that if we are simultaneously and ruthlessly destroying it.

Let's find ways to be faithful stewards today.

SHABBAT SHALOM

REFLECTION:

Do you have a biblical perspective on the environment and how we steward it?

.   .   .

WHAT ACTIONS CAN you take to be more 'sabbatical' in your approach (ie to be a better steward)?

45. DELIGHT

"If you keep your feet from breaking the Sabbath and from doing as you please on my holy day, if you call the Sabbath a delight and the Lord's holy day honourable, and if you honour it by not going your own way and not doing as you please or speaking idle words, then you will find your joy in the Lord"

— ISAIAH 58:13, 14 (NIV)

The Hebrew word translated as delight is *oneg*, and the concept of Oneg Shabbat has come to be important to Jewish people. It refers both to the delight Isaiah was talking about, and by extension has become the name of a gathering that takes place to celebrate the Sabbath.

Oneg Shabbat means that we actively choose to take pleasure in the Sabbath. It relates particularly to the physical enjoyment we take in the Sabbath, in eating, drinking, in sexual intimacy for a husband and wife, and so on.

It is one of the many ways we can understand the Jewish way of thinking as life affirming. God does not call us to detach ascetically from the world but to rightly engage with it.

IN FACT, rightly using the physical world to make the Sabbath an oasis of enjoyment is considered a holy and righteous thing to do, not a distraction from the business of pursuing God.

The verse says 'If...' So how can we learn to call the Sabbath a delight? What is it specifically on that day that will help us to feel this joy and wonder, this sense of delight?

Firstly, and simply, we must engage (sensibly) with those things that actually bring us pleasure, without feeling guilty or like we are being 'unspiritual' in some negative way.

This divide we have inherited between 'spiritual' and 'secular' can cause us to miss or dismiss much of the beauty of the life God has given us. Moreover the Sabbath itself was the first thing that God called holy.

Secondly, I think the key to finding joy is less in the things or people themselves and more about the vantage point from which we view them. The Sabbath helps us to see -

Children as a source of fun and innocence, not as a distraction from work or an inconvenience

Our spouse as our friend and partner in adventure - not someone we take for granted, or with whom we just share tasks

Food as a source of blessing and fellowship more than just fuel, and wine as more than just a sedative for a hard-pressed soul

Finances more as a source of blessing and possibility than just a means of paying the bills

Life as more than just accumulating and surviving and striving

---

Joy and delight come not from having everything we want but from realising we have all we need right now. And especially because ultimately all we need is found in God.

SABBATH IS a time to remember that *the joy of the Lord is our strength*.

To call the Sabbath a delight is a *choice* we have to make for ourselves. It will not force us, but God lovingly invites us.

In Jewish thinking the Sabbath is holy and blessed regardless of what we choose to do with it. But our engagement of it and experience is up to us, surely we would be foolish to miss out!

So let's call this Sabbath a delight and see where it takes us...

How do we begin to step into oneg shabbat? Simply find what brings us joy and makes us happy, spread this to others, and try to make the Sabbath a delight.

And as always – keep practicing!

SHABBAT SHALOM

REFLECTION:

WHAT DO you currently call the Sabbath?

WHAT CAN HELP you to make it a delight for you and your family?

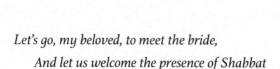

46. BRIDE

Let's go, my beloved, to meet the bride,
And let us welcome the presence of Shabbat

— FROM LECHAH DODI, TRADITIONAL
SONG SUNG AT THE SABBATH SERVICE

In Jewish thinking the Sabbath is likened to a bride and many of the thoughts and rituals that accompany it can be understood in this context. I want to consider three specific ideas -

Firstly, how is the Sabbath itself like a bride?

The sages say that creating the Sabbath was God's final act of creation, after creating the seen universe. He then married her to his newly created people, Israel, when he gave them his commandments at Sinai.

The Friday synagogue service is called the *Kabbalat*

Shabbat, which literally means *'receiving (or welcoming) the Sabbath'*. Many, especially orthodox Jewish people will even turn towards the door and bow as though to welcome her.

The term *Kabbalah* infers both a legal undertaking and the warmth of welcome and greeting. The Sabbath has both this legal sense of commitment and a personal sense of making room for intimacy.

This is precisely how we would describe a marriage - without commitment there is no security or integrity, without intimacy there is no heart or meaning.

The Sabbath is a loving commitment we take on ourselves. We welcome her as our bride, not out of duty but with the understanding that that she is intended for us and us for her.

THIS MEANS that at its heart the Sabbath is less a set of rules and regulations, and more associated with the delight and yearning of the Song of Solomon, the most intimate of all the books of the Bible.

Secondly, as believers we are also likened to a bride, the bride of Christ. Jesus yearns for us to be with him.

The Sabbath reminds us that we are not sterile rule keepers, we are the Messiah's treasured spouse, his reward and his confidante.

We provide a resting place for him and his father to come and make their home, and that is their desire. We are betrothed to him.

Thirdly, for those who are married the Sabbath is a key time in preserving and nurturing that relationship. There is a focus on intimacy and a sense of cherishing one another.

If we're parents the Sabbath helps us remember that we are first partners and lovers. Our union blesses and supports our children, so we must always nurture it.

In Jewish thought, the Sabbath is the time when the husband declares his love for and speaks blessings over his wife, expressing appreciation for all she does and is, and the gifts she brings during the week.

WITH TWO YOUNG children and Denise currently doing the lion's share of childcare, it's important for me to show appreciation rather than taking everything for granted.

However much I try to serve and accommodate around my work during the week, the Sabbath provides a time for me to express love and appreciation with actions not just words. For instance, giving her some space to rest properly away from the demands of looking after two boys, as well as time for us all together.

Every bride needs to feel cherished and loved in order to give her blessings back, in what is supposed to be a circle of love and delight. I don't always get there by any means, but it should be my aim!

If we think of the Sabbath in this way, it becomes a source of every form of intimacy -

It is our bride, promising a time of unhurried intimacy that the week can't offer.

It is a time to remember that we are his bride, and that he seeks intimacy with us.

It is a time to nurture intimacy with the ones we love, through time, service, and appreciation.

This Sabbath let's be conscious of all these aspects of what it means to place *bride* at the centre of our thinking rather than legalism.

SHABBAT SHALOM

—————

REFLECTION:

Do you see the Sabbath as a bride to be cherished or a duty?

Is the Sabbath a time to renew intimacy with God for you?

Wнo do you need to cherish and show love to this Sabbath?

47. PRESENT

And people should eat and drink and enjoy the fruits of their labour, for these are gifts from God.

— **ECCLESIASTES 3:13 (NLT)**

So I recommend having fun, because there is nothing better for people in this world than to eat, drink, and enjoy life.

— **ECCLESIASTES 8:15 (NLT)**

The Sabbath teaches us to live in the moment, to be present with those closest to us. If ever there was a time we needed to learn that lesson it is now.

I need to learn it with my wife – to nurture our love and keep our hearts as close as they can be.

I need to learn it with my children – to treasure the moments in each precious season, to remind myself that being present means sowing time and my full attention to reap a harvest of relationship with them in later years, and to build their confidence for the journey that lies before them.

The Sabbath reminds us that -

The only time we ever have is the current moment. It sounds obvious but sometimes we need to stop and let that sink in.

I SPEND TOO much time trying to make sense of the past, to reclaim things that were lost, or rekindle fires I think have grown colder. I spend too much time living in the future and imagining what me and my efforts might amount to one day.

But the truth is success and failure, joy and misery, are determined by the use I make of *now*, of each moment, and the way I use my present to grow and step forward.

Why do the simplest things seem to often be the hardest? Our hurried and harried souls tend to resist this idea of living in the present.

We drag the past around like a chain and accumulate imaginary successes for the future through fear or fantasy. Letting go of this takes courage, for it has become our security.

The Sabbath helps us to let go of this way of being and to live in the present.

If meditation is the deliberate focusing of the whole self on the now, then the Sabbath is like a twenty-four-hour meditation.

To be present is at the heart of loving God, self, and others. We cannot give of ourselves if our mind and heart is occupied elsewhere.

WHEN WE LEARN *to be present with ourselves and God we can begin to be present with those closest to us.*

Am I present with my children? Fully alive with them?

Am I present with my spouse? Do I give my whole heart?

What about God? A Sunday service cannot teach you to be present with God, yourself, or others. Often it is a deception to imagine it can.

The Sabbath teaches us how to let go of past and future and rest in the current moment.

To not put off enjoying what we have until tomorrow. To not wait until we have all our ducks in a row or that goal we have been chasing, but to simply let go of everything that is a burden and be present to the moment.

I can be like that – rationing my enjoyment for those achievements I think merit it. But Sabbath says *now*. Enjoy today, for it is – ALWAYS – all we have. The important moment is not later or another, more significant day, but now.

And as Walter Bruggerman said, those who live the Sabbath differently tend to live the other six days differently also.

I think we need to let the Sabbath teach us about how to live life fully every day, how to carry this sense of being present into the week.

If we learn these lessons our lives will become more beautiful, and gratitude, praise, and generosity more natural responses.

So this Sabbath, let's try and come back to enjoying the moment for what it is and being fully present for those around us.

SHABBAT SHALOM

PRESENT

*R*EFLECTION:

*H*OW PRESENT ARE *you in the moments of your life?*

*H*OW PRESENT ARE *you for those closest to you?*

*H*OW ABLE ARE *you to enjoy the blessings that God has given you?*

48. SPIRIT

He who is slow to anger is better than the mighty, And he who rules his spirit than he who takes a city.

— PROVERBS 16:32,33 (NKJV)

The Sabbath teaches us to rule our spirit. It gives us a space to learn what it means to manage ourselves well.

The idea of somebody who rules their spirit is somebody who is self-aware. Someone who knows themselves well enough to handle their emotions, their decisions, and their thought life.

To manage any organisation or community you have to understand how the different elements work, and how they fit together. The same is true of ourselves. The Sabbath gives us space to help us reflect and learn.

The Bible tells us that learning to be like this is a greater accomplishment than external success, even conquering a city. That is why God provides a space each week to practice, and insists his people take up the offer! It's as though he says - I know you, and trust me, you need this!

Jesus shared a similar thought - *'For what profit is it to a man if he gains the whole world, and loses his own soul?'* (Matt. 16:26 NKJV)

We cannot expect to accomplish great things and win the battles of life unless we are willing to pay some attention to the battle within and the seemingly 'little' things.

HOW THEN DO we actually rule our own spirit? Two thoughts -

Firstly, we maintain a sense of God's presence at the centre of our lives. We do not allow ourselves to be tossed to this side or that or drawn away with our thoughts.

We bring everything into subjection to God's order, yielding the offending and broken areas to him.

Romans 8:6 (NLT) puts it this way - *'So letting your sinful nature control your mind leads to death. But letting the Spirit control your mind leads to life and peace'.*

We cannot rule our spirits simply by our own efforts at self-discipline or positive thinking. Instead we need to ask for God's help, to allow him to speak, to guide us to the truth, to bring peace where there are storms and confusion.

Secondly, we must learn to know our own hearts and keep acknowledging areas and patterns that we know are dysfunctional.

As we give God access to these we find a transformation taking place. He is like the 'dent magician' for our lives – His presence sucks the dents out so we return to the shape he designed.

Only as we allow the prince of peace to govern our hearts can we learn to rule our spirits and operate from a place of peace ourselves.

THINGS CAN GET PRETTY unruly in my mind and in my heart, and I'm sure you're the same! So this Sabbath let's take some time to surrender to God and give him victory in our hearts.

As we do we can begin to rule our spirits.

Then we take the city! Roll on Monday! But for now -

SHABBAT SHALOM

REFLECTION:

IN WHAT AREAS do you need to learn to rule your spirit more?

WHAT AREAS FEEL out of control?

HOW CAN you yield them to God more today?

49. JESUS

> *And He said to them, "The Sabbath was made for man, and not man for the Sabbath. Therefore the Son of Man is also Lord of the Sabbath."*

> — **MARK 2:27,28 (NKJV)**

Somehow Christians have often taken this verse to mean Jesus cancelled or minimised the Sabbath - he is *'Lord of the Sabbath'* so if he wants to throw it away or bend the rules he will! (And because it is 'Old Testament' he probably does..)

I think this is a misinterpretation and misunderstanding of what Jesus was saying.

To start with it would make him a hypocrite – one moment telling people to obey God's commandments, the next disobeying and ignoring them himself.

Secondly, Jesus could only die for our sins because

he was perfect and hadn't broken the commandments. This must include the Sabbath.

And let's be clear, neither Jesus nor his disciples called anything 'the Old Testament' – they called the Scriptures 'the Law and the prophets', 'the Word of God', 'the Holy writings' – and so on.

Everything they taught about faith, love, and the promises of God is found in them.

———

Jesus lived the Sabbath his whole life and expected his followers to do the same. There is no record of him ignoring or breaking the Sabbath or teaching us to.

———

WHAT HE DID DO WAS CLARIFY its *purpose* and *outworking*. He demonstrated that healing is a good thing, and that work is not defined by pernickety detailed instructions.

He taught and showed us that it's through the lens of love that we need to view the Sabbath, not the endless addition of rules and regulations, because as he says in the verse above, it was made for us not the other way around!

But - *he never cancelled it.*

Think of this - what part of the Torah did Jesus suggest we should dial down on? Which of the Ten Commandments did he say we could mess with a little bit now we were 'under grace'? Can we murder a little bit? Commit a bit of adultery? No!

The message of Jesus is that we must go beyond the minimum.

Beyond not murdering to actually loving. Beyond not committing adultery to actually becoming pure hearted. We must live the fullness of the Word so it becomes flesh in us.

In addition to the forgiveness of sins, Jeremiah described the coming new covenant in this manner *'I will put my law in their minds and write it on their hearts'* (Jeremiah 31:33 NKJV). Jesus made the way for this to happen.

So we must go beyond not working on the Sabbath to actually finding deep rest for our souls, actually releasing the pursuit of the world's goals from our hearts.

WE MUST LIVE the *intent* of the Sabbath, as well as the actions, if our righteousness is to exceed that of the Pharisees.

My yoke is easy and my burden is light means that Jesus has an interpretation of the commandments that will truly allow us to flourish. Two oxen were yoked together to pull a plough, and Jesus says come and be yoked with me, feel the rhythm by which I carry myself and learn to do the same.

To observe the Sabbath is no more legalistic than going to church at a regular time each week, praying at a particular time each day, or working your way through a Bible reading plan. Legalism is not in the action, it is in the motive.

AS WE HAVE SEEN, stepping into the Sabbath rest truly is an act of faith. And it is a time for believers to remember that Jesus alone - the Lord of the Sabbath - is our Lord. We can rest because we are yoked to him, forgiven and walking at his unhurried pace.

As his disciples he wants to teach and train us. If he has become our Lord and we have chosen to follow him, then the Sabbath is a weekly reminder of who he is, and also a part of our training.

If Jesus is one with his father then just as the father rested on the seventh day, after creation, so Jesus would also - for Jesus is the image of God. And if so, then so should we.

The Sabbath brings us back to Jesus, it's a time to remember he is with us and he is all we need.

So this Sabbath let's keep it simple – the Lord of the

Sabbath saves, delivers, redeems, heals, and restores our souls.

I am my beloved's and he is mine. Let's remember that we are yoked to him – the Lord of the Sabbath and the light of our lives.

SHABBAT SHALOM

REFLECTION:

WHAT DO *you think Jesus means when he says he is Lord of the Sabbath?*

IN WHAT WAYS, *if at all, do you associate Jesus with the Sabbath?*

HOW CAN *the Sabbath help you draw closer to Jesus?*

50. SHALOM

Peace I leave with you, My peace I give to you; not as the world gives do I give to you. Let not your heart be troubled, neither let it be afraid.

— JOHN 14:27 (NKJV)

Why didn't I just translate the word and call this week's reflection 'peace'? The answer is that shalom means so much more than just peace, especially in the way we think of peace.

Each week I sign off '*Shabbat shalom*', the greeting Jewish people say to one another on the Sabbath. So let's look at what shalom actually means.

Shalom is the sense of wholeness, completeness, that is more than an absence of conflict or strife. Shalom carries a sense of richness and abundance in our souls.

SHALOM

More than an absence of waves, shalom is a sense of contentment in the midst of whatever is going on, however turbulent. It is a sense of unbroken connection with God, self, and others.

WHEN JESUS SAID *'my peace I leave you'* he didn't mean troubles would disappear and all would be plain sailing and easy! He meant he was leaving them with *his* shalom, a true unshakeable peace that would sustain them through the struggles and persecution, including any injustice they would face. The same peace that carried him through a world of troubles.

This is the mistake people make when they say, *'If the Messiah has come, how come there isn't peace on Earth?'* The answer is that Jesus isn't interested in an imposed, static peace that means no activity. That's why sometimes he calmed the waves but other times he calmed the disciples' hearts in the *midst* of the waves.

There is a peace that is growing here on Earth, but it is growing in the hearts of his disciples as they learn to become more and more like him, building his kingdom and demonstrating it to the world. It is in their relationships with one another and what they are called to bring to the world.

Shalom means that the Prince of peace is present and reigning.

Shalom manifests in our relationships - we are commanded to seek to live peaceably with others. Yet it starts first in our relationship with God. The Bible tells us that we can have peace with God through what Jesus did for us.

Too few of us understand or live in the full significance of what that really means. If we did we wouldn't experience that nagging sense of failure or condemnation that often seems to haunt us.

But the more we understand shalom with God, the more we begin to allow this peace to enter our hearts and take root in the core of our being.

Shalom carries the sense of 'nothing broken, nothing missing'. When we allow God to work in our hearts, and his word to become flesh in us, then we can begin to experience the fullness of life we are supposed to have in God.

AND THE SABBATH gives us a picture and an experience of what this shalom might look like -

On the Sabbath we bask in our shalom with God.

We experience a sense of shalom in our souls.

And we experience a sense of shalom in our families and communities.

It is this sense of wholeness and communion that causes the rabbis to call the Sabbath a taste of the Messiah's kingdom to come, where there will be no conflict or striving.

Experiencing this in practice often means actually letting go of our attempts to calm every storm and fix every situation, and instead reminding ourselves that true shalom can only be found in one place – the Prince of shalom!

So this Sabbath, let's enjoy a taste of eternity as we rest. Not the absence of all trouble but a sense of well-being and the presence of God and one another.

SHABBAT SHALOM

REFLECTION:

WHERE DO you need God's shalom today?

WHAT DO you need to let go of so you can you receive more shalom in your soul?

51. GOOD

> '*Then God saw everything that He had made, and indeed it was very good. So the evening and the morning were the sixth day.*'

> — GENESIS 1:31 (NKJV)

The Sabbath followed God's declaration that his creation is good.

The goodness of the creation is a reflection of the creator's goodness, for it is imbued with his characteristics, built by one who is defined by the word love.

The Sabbath is introduced as an expression both of God's goodness and of the goodness of creation. The rabbis say that God looked at creation and saw what was missing - then he created the Sabbath.

The serpent's insinuations in the garden of Eden are

intended to undermine this sense of the goodness of God.

First, he questions God's character - did God *really* say, '*you must not eat the fruit from any of the trees in the garden?*' By this he twists God's expansive '*you may eat of all the trees except...*' and introduces the idea of a restrictive, repressive God.

Then he suggests God is lying about the one tree and death, and casts him as an insecure and anxious God, worried in case his creation becomes too like him and knows what he knows.

Whilst none of this could be further from the truth, the question that it implies is this – *is God really good?*

And this is the question that still resounds today, in every doubt, fear, challenging circumstance - *is God good?*

When sickness comes, is he good? When financial struggles are present, is he good? When I don't get the promotion I wanted, the partner I wanted, or the path I wanted - *is he good*? But -

The Sabbath stands forever as a ringing bell, a repeated weekly declaration of the goodness of God in the face of our doubts and challenges.

GOD RESTS because he is satisfied that he has imbued his creation with his goodness and he wants to both enjoy it, and to be enjoyed for the good God that he is.

With the stain and damage of that first sin and all its consequences washed away by the sacrifice of Jesus on the cross, we can now truly enjoy the Sabbath as it was intended to be – a gift of time between a loving creator and his creation.

The land rests, the animals rest, and we all, as one - God's children - rest as well, reflecting on his goodness towards us and amongst us, unifying us.

The Sabbath is set apart as holy for this very reason – it proclaims God's goodness to his creation.

UNDERSTOOD in this light Jesus's rebuke to the Pharisees makes perfect sense. They had turned the Sabbath into an expression of a restrictive and anxious God, the image of the serpent's lie. They had turned the Sabbath into the exact opposite of what God intended it to be – an expression of his *goodness* towards us.

Instead Jesus restored the Sabbath as the gift and blessing of a generous, secure, loving God who wants to heal, restore, and nourish his people.

He did this both by teaching on the subject, and by associating his healing ministry with the Sabbath –

more of Jesus' miracles took place on that day than any other, as though he was placing a special stamp of approval on it.

Jesus restored the Sabbath as that declaration of God's goodness, and God's belief in the goodness of his creation.

This Sabbath, and every Sabbath, let's remind ourselves of both these truths. And let's allow them to become core beliefs at the heart of who we are.

The Sabbath used correctly is one of our best weapons in the struggle for truth and love to prevail in the world.

SHABBAT SHALOM

REFLECTION:

How do you see the Sabbath - as the gift of a good God or the restrictive command of a demanding one?

Take a few minutes, or longer, to reflect on and meditate on God's goodness towards you

52. GOD

On the seventh day God had finished his work of creation, so he rested from all his work. And God blessed the seventh day and declared it holy, because it was the day when he rested from all his work of creation.

— GENESIS 2:1-3 (NLT)

Your Bible tells you that God rested on the seventh day but in fact this is a little misleading.

To rest sounds quite passive but the Hebrew actually says that God *sabbathed* on that day. The best translation for this is in fact that God stopped what he was doing. The emphasis is more on arrival at a destination, the finishing of what came before.

Which begs the question, why did God stop creating at this point?

God's stopping points to a sense of reaching a

purposed aim. We see that at the end of the sixth day *'God looked over all he had made and he saw that it was very good!'*

The majesty of creation is replaced by something much more intimate - the God who enjoys his creation.

God doesn't stand outside but *responds* to his creation. He enters into relationship with it, on and through the Sabbath.

And as Karl Barth said, *'the reason why he refrains from further activity on the seventh day is that he has found the object of his love and has no need for any further works'.*

God's enjoyment of the Sabbath is specifically an expression of his love for you and me, and his desire to be involved in our lives rather than stand apart as a creator.

HE NO LONGER NEEDS TO CREATE BECAUSE he is satisfied with what he has created and wants to enjoy interacting with it.

He knows the journey will be 'interesting' (ie complicated and messy) because he knows the beginning from the end. He knows all things. And yet he says it is worth it, and you and I are enough.

Whatever imperfections may enter his creation, whatever troubles lie ahead, the God who created the universe declares that it is good and that he will be involved, by this action of arriving on the Sabbath.

Whenever we are tempted to think that God has forgotten us or find ourselves overwhelmed by life's challenges and the urgency of each day's problems, then *we must remember the Sabbath!*

It stands as a marker, a reminder each week of this incredible truth – that *God is still invested in our lives, still in love with us, still passionate to be our everything just as we are his.*

The seventh day is not just an afterthought, a pause between bouts of creation, or just a time to refresh, however much it may fulfil all those purposes and more.

It is at heart an expression of God's desire to have fellowship with his creation. The gift is one based less on *function* and more on *relationship.* As though God is saying, *now that the work is done let's take time to acknowledge and enjoy one another. For this was the purpose of it all, and the seventh day the pinnacle.*

The fact that God initiated the Sabbath means he offers it to us as a gift, not a burden. How we choose to use it is up to us. But the offer is there, God's graceful arms outstretched in welcome and desire.

WILL we choose to use it as a reminder, and a haven in which we come back to the *why* behind it all - to love God and love one another as we love ourselves? To enjoy life. Or will we leave it languishing on the shelf?

Through the course of these reflections I have tried to unpack and unwrap this gift in every manner possible so that we can understand its beauty, appreciate its variety of uses, and take advantage of its practical benefits for our lives.

Yet there is still so much more to the multi-faceted jewel of the Sabbath. Still so much to discover in the different layers.

This fifty second Sabbath, I pray you would have such a revelation of how this gift can enhance your life, family, and community, that you would always get the most you can out of it.

May you experience God's shalom each week as you 'sabbath', just as God did. May you experience his joy or 'oneg Shabbat'. And may you find his life at work in you like never before.

SHABBAT SHALOM

REFLECTION:

.   .   .

Do you see the Sabbath as a gift from God made for you?

How will you keep it in that place and use it from now on?

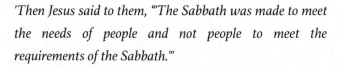

53. POSTSCRIPT

'Then Jesus said to them, "'The Sabbath was made to meet the needs of people and not people to meet the requirements of the Sabbath.'"

— MARK 2:27 (NLT)

We have come to the end of our series of reflections on *how* the Sabbath helps meet our needs -

THE SABBATH LOOKS BACK -
    To creation
    To the Exodus
    To the wilderness

THE SABBATH IS **present** -

It gives a new reality and paradigm for twenty-four hours

It encourages a sense of living in the now

THE SABBATH LOOKS FORWARD -
To the reign of the Messiah
To God's kingdom on the earth
To a time of complete justice and peace

THE SABBATH LOOKS **up** -
To God who created us

THE SABBATH LOOKS **in** -
To our own well-being and identity

THE SABBATH LOOKS **out** -
To how we are treating others and the community we are building to represent God

THE SABBATH IS a multi-purpose tool and a multi-faceted jewel that God has given us. It is a matrix or tesseract rather than a blunt instrument.

The imperative command contains the narrative also - it is an instruction that is tied to our story, both past, present and future.

The Sabbath reminds us what to do today, but also what has happened in the past, and what will happen in the future.

It is like love - simple as an idea, but yet so rich in meaning it cannot be reduced to a simple task or feeling.

It develops and grows as we unfold it, taking new and changing shapes, asking and answering questions we never quite realised we needed to ask.

If we let it, it will help us, guide us, and serve us well. It has not been replaced or reduced. Simply unpacked and explained.

It is a gift we would do well to use in its fullness, as it waits for us and welcomes us.

SHABBAT SHALOM,
David

ALSO BY DAVID HOFFBRAND

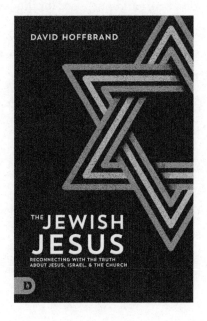

The Jewish Jesus, Reconnecting with the truth about Jesus, Israel, and the church - published by Destiny Image

What relevance does it have that Jesus is Jewish and what difference should it make to our faith?

In *The Jewish Jesus*, David Hoffbrand explores the answers to these and related questions in a way that is accessible to everyone.

As you see how Jesus lived, thought and taught as a Jewish man, you will come to know Him like never before, and find that His teachings come alive in their original context.

This book will also help you:

· Appreciate the Jewish context of the whole Bible, reconnecting the Old and New Testaments

· Rediscover God's heart and purposes for the Jewish people and Israel

· Engage with God's blueprint for the church as a unified but diverse community of believers

· Learn principles that will help you restore the Jewish "lens" in a way that enriches your faith

DISCOVER THE JEWISH JESUS!

Available through Amazon and all other booksellers

ABOUT THE AUTHOR

David Hoffbrand grew up in a Jewish family in north London, and has a passion to see the church reconnect with the Jewish Jesus and the Jewish framework for understanding the Bible.

David's previous book, *The Jewish Jesus - Reconnecting with the truth about Jesus, Israel, and the church*, helps people to have an understanding of these three areas and how they all relate.

David and his wife Denise live in Brighton, England, with their sons Isaac and Levi. They are part of the oversight at CityCoast Church, a church of INC (International Network of Churches).

David is a trustee for Maoz Uk, and The David House, with whom he works in Ukraine and other countries to develop One New Man networks of

Messianic rabbis and pastors together. He is also part of the Towards Jerusalem Council 2 (TJC2) Uk team.

David has a BSc in Psychology and a Masters in Social Work. He previously worked as a social worker alongside various roles within the church, where he helps in areas of discipleship and inner wholeness.

David is also a singer-songwriter and has released three albums.

For further information visit:

www.davidhoffbrand.com

www.facebook.com/davidhoffbrand

www.instagram.com/davidhoffbrand

Printed in Great Britain
by Amazon

43734567R00149